BYRON

Detail from the painting by VINCENZO CAMUCCINI
Galleria di S. Luca, Rome

BYRON

II. LITERARY SATIRE, HUMOUR AND REFLECTION

by

BERNARD BLACKSTONE

Edited by Ian Scott-Kilvert

PUBLISHED FOR
THE BRITISH COUNCIL
BY LONGMAN GROUP LTD

LONGMAN GROUP LTD
Longman House, Burnt Mill, Harlow, Essex

*Associated companies, branches and
representatives throughout the world*

First published 1971
© Bernard Blackstone 1971

*Printed in Great Britain by
F. Mildner & Sons, London, EC1*

SBN 0 582 01219 8

BYRON

I. INTRODUCTION

GEORGE GORDON, later to be the sixth Lord Byron, was born in London on 22 January 1788 and died at Missolonghi on 19 April 1824. His mother, Catherine Gordon, was a Scottish heiress descended from the Stuarts; his father, Captain John ('Mad Jack') Byron, nephew of the fifth or 'wicked' Lord Byron and son of Admiral John Byron (1723-1786) traced his long line of scapegrace forebears back to the Ernegis and Radulfus de Burun who had come over with William the Conqueror. A history of violence runs through both the maternal and the paternal line of Byron's family.

Captain John Byron's first marriage had been to the Marchioness of Carmarthen after her divorce from the Marquis in 1779; Byron's half-sister Augusta was the only surviving child of this marriage. Whether or not Mad Jack ill-treated his wife, as some said but Byron later denied ('It is not by "brutality" that a young officer in the Guards seduces and carries off a Marchioness, and marries two heiresses'), she died in January 1784, and her £4,000 a year departed with her; the Captain had to look round again. He met Catherine Gordon of Bight, a girl of twenty with an estate worth more than £23,000, at Bath, and married her in May 1785. He rapidly ran through her fortune and decamped to France to avoid his creditors. He returned to England in time for the birth of his son in 1788, but was back in France by September 1790; whence he wrote to his sister on 16 February 1791: 'With regard to Mrs Byron, I am glad she writes to you. She is very amiable at a distance; but I defy you and all the Apostles to live with her two months, for, if any body could live with her, it was me . . . For my son, I am happy to hear he is well; but for his walking, 'tis impossible, as he is club-footed.' Captain Byron died on 2 August 1791.

The club-footed poet was brought up by his neurotic mother in Aberdeen, after their removal from London in 1789, in what used to be called 'straitened circumstances'. He had a lower-middle-class education at 'a School kept by a Mr *Bowers*, who was called "*Bodsy* Bowers" by reason of his dapperness. It was a School for both sexes. I learned little there, except to repeat by rote the first lesson of Monosyllables—"God made man, let us love him" . . . ' It is tempting to speculate what Byron's future might have been but for the cannon-ball which removed the fifth lord's grandson from the succession to the title in 1794. Lord Byron's own death at Newstead on 21 May 1798 meant George Gordon's accession to the peerage, to Newstead Abbey, and to the many debts incurred by the 'wicked lord'. Byron and his mother settled in at Newstead in August 1798.

There were three years of residence at Newstead, of neighbourly visits (Mary Chaworth, his first love, lived next door at Annesley Hall), of attendance at Dr Glennie's school in Dulwich. In 1801 came the removal to public school life at Harrow. In 1805 he went up to Trinity, Cambridge, where he did little work but made a number of friends and prepared his first volume of poems, *Hours of Idleness*, for the press. From this point onwards the incidents of his life are so closely interwoven with his writing that all I need give here is a skeleton survey, to be filled up in detail as we follow his career as a poet.

Hours of Idleness appeared in June 1807 and was contemptuously noticed by *The Edinburgh Review* of January 1808. 'As an author, I am cut to atoms by the E. Review', he wrote in a letter of 27 February; 'it is just out, and has completely demolished my little fabric of fame . . .' He replied with *English Bards and Scotch Reviewers* (March 1809), a brilliant and devastating satire; and set out (2 July 1809) for the Continent. He travelled through Portugal and Spain, Greece and Asia Minor, returning to Britain in July 1811 with the first two cantos of *Childe Harold* in his portmanteau.

Published in March 1812, the new poem had an immediate success: on the morrow of its appearance he notes, 'I awoke to find myself famous'. This extraordinary fame, greater perhaps than any other poet has enjoyed in his lifetime, endured to the end of his life and beyond. He became the idol of London high society, and his amours, particularly that with Lady Caroline Lamb, were notorious. *Childe Harold* was followed in the years from 1813 to 1816 by the succession of Oriental (and other) Tales, beginning with *The Giaour* (May 1813) and ending with *The Prisoner of Chillon* (Dec. 1816) which confirmed his standing as the foremost of European poets.

In 1809 he took his seat in the House of Lords, and on 27 February 1812 made his maiden speech, opposing a bill which specified the death penalty for frame breaking. On 2 January 1815 he married the blue-stocking heiress Annabella Milbanke. The marriage was not a happy one, and there were scandals about Byron's relationship with his half-sister Augusta and his homosexual tendencies; a daughter, Ada, was born in 1815, but in March 1816 a legal separation was agreed upon and in April Byron left England for ever.

Eight years of life remained to him. They were filled with feverish creative activity—the second part of *Childe Harold* (Canto III, published in November 1816, Canto IV, published in April 1818), the dramas, the enormous panorama of *Don Juan*. He formed the last and most important of his friendships, with Shelley; the first meeting was at Geneva in May 1816, and the acquaintance deepened as the two poets pursued their curious interlacing orbits through the length and breadth of Italy from 1818 to 1822.

The Italian years were filled with many adventures, but Byron's last real attachment of a heterosexual kind was to Teresa, the nineteen-year-old wife of the fifty-eight-year old Count Alessandro Guiccioli, who remained his mistress until his final journey to Greece. They met in Venice in 1819; the curious sexual *mores* of Italy at this period made it possible for Byron to reside in the Count's palace as *cavalier servente* of the Countess ('What shall I do? I am in love, and tired of promiscuous concubinage, and have now an opportunity of settling for life.') There were difficulties, however (it is possible to be too famous for comfort); the legal separation of the Guicciolis, sojourn of Teresa under her parental roof, reunion, quarrels over *Don Juan*, which Teresa thought too cynical. The scene shifts from Venice to Ravenna, from Ravenna to Pisa. Love is interspersed with fights and with political plotting for the freedom of Italy, saddened by the death of his illegitimate daughter Allegra. 'Awful work, this love', Byron comments ruefully in a letter to Tom Moore of 19 September 1821.

But soon the awful work was to be over for ever. The Greek war of independence, simmering for decades, broke into open flame in 1821. Shelley wrote his stirring drama, *Hellas*. English philhellenes formed a London Committee for the promotion of the Greek cause. All eyes turned to Byron, the greatest living philhellene, and when in 1822 he was approached by the London Greek Committee he was not slow to respond. In all his wanderings his heart and mind had remained faithful to the land which, as he had long ago declared, had 'made him a poet . . . a land it is a privilege even to have visited'—which, when even its memory passes for a moment across his page, lifts it 'into sudden blaze', so that the mere recollection of 'those magical and memorable abodes' (*Childe Harold* IV, Dedication) is sufficient to fill his verse with subtlety and sweetness. Byron sailed for Greece on 24 July 1823; after a stay in Cephalonia, then a British protectorate, he arrived at Missolonghi in January 1824. He died there of fever on 19 April 1824. His remains, which the Greeks wished to inter in the Temple of Theseus in Athens, were transported to England, refused a burial in Westminster Abbey, and finally laid to rest by the side of the 'wicked lord' in the family vault in Hucknall Torkard church. Perhaps his best requiem was reported by the peasant poet John Clare, who in his later madness fancied himself to be Byron and composed a new *Childe Harold*. He is writing in his 1824 journal:

I was wandering up Oxford Street on my way to Mrs Emmerson's when my eye was suddenly arrested by straggling groups of the common people collected together & talking about a funeral I did as the rest did though I could not get hold of what funeral it could be but I knew it was not a common one by the curiosity that kept watch on every countenance. By & by the group collected into about a hundred or more when the train of a funeral suddenly appeared on which a young girl that stood beside me gave a deep sigh & uttered 'Poor Lord Byron'.

II. THE LITERARY SATIRES

English Bards and Scotch Reviewers (1809) was Byron's answer to the *Edinburgh Review's* contemptuous dismissal of his first volume of verse, the *Hours of Idleness* (1807). The critique had wounded him deeply. 'He was very near destroying himself', his friend Hobhouse reports, perhaps with some exaggeration. In his journal five years later Byron reminisces: 'I . . . read it the day of its denunciation— dined and drank three bottles of claret (with S. B. Davies, I think), neither ate nor slept the less, but, nevertheless, was not easy till I had vented my wrath and my rhyme, in the same pages, against every thing and every body . . .'

Byron's first full-length satire is in Pope's couplet and to some extent in Pope's manner, though it lacks the polished urbanity of 'the little Queen Anne's man'. Its rasp and occasional buffoonery betray the influence of the mock-epic satirists closer to Byron's own day, notably of Gifford in his *Baviad* and *Mæviad* (1794–5). In tone and lay-out it is astonishingly original, shot through and through with the Byronic attributes of gusto, humour, sheer farce and wry magnanimity so alien to the great Popean virtues of moderation, decorum, virulent understatement, and sym- metry. In what follows I shall be discussing Byron's first satire not simply as a detached poem, but in the context of his total outlook in the years 1807-9, pressing into service moreover material in his later journals.

Wit, humour, farce, spleen—the poem moves through a gamut of tones. Byron's wit is a facet of his eighteenth-century heritage, his descent from Dryden and Pope and Johnson, and beyond them from Sedley and Rochester. It is closer to Rochester and Dryden in its energy and large carelessness, to Pope in its mordancy and scope. It is more genial than Pope's, however. Byron does not spare his victims, but he is seldom bitter. Laughing at others, he takes the occasion to laugh at himself:

> No Muse will cheer, with renovating smile,
> The paralytic puling of CARLISLE . . .   (725-6)

(where the mild absurdity of 'renovating smile' clashes with the ferocity of 'paralytic puling' to produce an 'æsthetic shock')—yes, but:

> Lords too are Bards: such things at times befall,
> And 'tis some praise in Peers to write at all.   (719-20)

Through it all there runs a stream of fun-making, of farce, a revelling in the incongruous. Assailing one of the most egregious, if harmless, of the age's poetasters, Coleridge's bookseller friend Amos Cottle (1768?-1800), Byron distils the maximum of amusement out of his victim's name.

> Oh, AMOS COTTLE!—Phoebus! what a name
> To fill the speaking-trump of future fame!—
> Oh, AMOS COTTLE! for a moment think
> What meagre profits spring from pen and ink!
> When thus devoted to poetic dreams,
> Who will peruse thy prostituted reams?
> Oh, pen perverted! paper misapplied!
> Had COTTLE still adorned the counter's side,
> Bent o'er the desk, or, born to useful toils,
> Been taught to make the paper which he soils,
> Ploughed, delved, or plied the oar with lusty limb,
> He had not sung of Wales, nor I of him.   (399-410)

Now this may strike us as cruel and snobbish, the noble lord assailing a tradesman. But that is not the point. Byron had no contempt for tradesmen or ploughmen if they wrote good poetry, as he recognized Burns did, and Bloomfield. But he objected to bad poetry from Cottle as much as from the Earl of Carlisle; and what amused him about Cottle was the name. This would not have amused Dryden or Pope: it belongs to Byron's Shakespearian side, his love for puns, for word-play, for ludicrous rhymes.[1] His mock-Milton catalogue of odd-sounding proper names in *Don Juan* VII, xvi–xvii, is a later example.

Schoolboy humour, perhaps. There's a lot of it in Byron, and particularly in the letters, for which his first editor and biographer, Tom Moore, makes solemn apology. But what to Moore seemed unworthy the dignity of a major poet strikes us today as the kind of informality, ease and naturalness we look for from someone of the stature of Shakespeare or Byron, someone not concerned with making an effect. And with it goes a kind of humility. The Letters and Journals show Byron laughing at himself, at his ambiguous fame:

Murray (Byron's publisher) has had a letter from his brother bibliopole of Edinburgh, who says, 'he is lucky in having such a poet'—something as if one was a packhorse, or 'ass or anything that is his'; or, like Mrs Packwood, who replied to some enquiry after the Ode on Razors— 'Lawks, sir, we *keeps* a poet'. The same illustrious Edinburgh bookseller once sent an order for books, poesy, and cookery, with this agreeable postscript—'The *Harold* and *Cookery* are much wanted.' Such is fame . . .
(Journal, 13 Dec. 1813)

This is that 'wisdom of sheer roguish pranks which', as Nietzsche says about Socrates, 'constitutes the best state of soul in a man'. It is the voice of our non-Romantic Byron, with the keenest of noses for the ridiculous, the slyest eye for

[1] Wilkes's jibe at Elkanah Settle in Boswell's *Life of Johnson* is the direct ancestor of this, and Arnold found similar ammunition in 'Wragg': '. . . has anyone reflected what a touch of grossness in our race . . . is shown by the natural growth among us of such hideous names—Higginbottom, Stiggins, Bugg?' (*Essays in Criticism*, I, 'The Function of Criticism').

his own status in an hierarchy which includes Homer and
Horace, Shakespeare and Dante. 'How I do delight in
observing life as it really is!—and myself, after all, the worst
of any', he exclaims a little later in this 1813–14 journal,
'But no matter—I must avoid egotism, which, just now,
would be no vanity'. It is precisely this observation of life
as it is, with all its curious quirks and quibbles, that gives
Byron's humour its strength and resilience.

Byron detested stereotypes, took delight in odd personali-
ties, in the little lunacies that break the mould. We understand him best on this side if we see him as one of the last of
the great English eccentrics, keeping a pet bear in his rooms
at Trinity ('Sir, I mean him to sit for a fellowship' was his
reply to his tutor's plaintive demurrer), peopling his
Venetian palace with a collection (according to Shelley) of
three monkeys, eight mastiffs, five peacocks, five cats, one
eagle, one crow, one falcon, two guinea hens, one wolf and
an Egyptian crane; boxing with Cribb or Jackson in the
intervals of writing his Eastern romances, enjoying bacon-
and-eggs and beer at one moment and *haute cuisine* at
another, he qualifies for the judgement he himself passed on
Burns: 'What an antithetical mind! tenderness, roughness
—sentiment, sensuality—soaring and grovelling, dirt and
deity—all mixed up in that one compound of inspired clay!'
This was the Byron from whom his fellow Romantics, and
later Victorians, averted their eyes.

I wonder how the deuce anybody could make such a world—for what
purposes dandies, for instance, were ordained—and kings—and fellows
of colleges—and women of 'a certain age'—and men of any age—and
myself, most of all! . . . is there anything beyond?—*who* knows? *He*
that can't tell. Who tells that there *is*? He who don't know. And when
shall he know? perhaps, when he don't expect, and generally when he
don't wish it. In this last respect, however, all are not alike: it depends a
good deal upon education—something upon nerves and habits—but
most upon digestion.

Thus Byron in his journal for 18 February 1814. It's not
complex or profound, it's just an intelligent and thoughtful

man mulling things over without any preconceptions about a 'Wisdom and Spirit of the Universe' or an 'Intellectual Beauty'; trying to worry things out on the small basis of fact we are, in fact, given. Reading his private journal we feel ourselves to be in the presence of an agile and in many ways a subtle mind. Byron the man comes to life for us as he sat night after night at his desk in his rooms in Albany or his palace at Ravenna, his journal open before him and a glass of hock or madeira at his elbow. Let us eavesdrop a little further. Solitude—is it good for one, he ponders?

Redde a little—wrote notes and letters, and am alone, which Locke says is bad company. 'Be not solitary, be not idle.'—Um!—the idleness is troublesome; but I can't see so much to regret in the solitude. The more I see of men, the less I like them. If I could but say so of women too, all would be well. Why can't I? I am now six-and-twenty; my passions have had enough to cool them; my affections more than enough to wither them—and yet—and yet—always *yet* and *but*—'Excellent well, you are a fishmonger—get thee to a nunnery'.—'They fool me to the top of my bent'.

There we have Byron the cynic and misanthropist. We think we have pinned down our butterfly. But then suddenly there emerges another Byron—equally voluble, equally 'humorous': the man of energy who is also the divided mind, the split soul:

No letters today—so much the better—there are no answers. I must not dream again—it spoils even reality. I will go out of doors, and see what the fog will do for me. Jackson has been here: the boxing world much as usual. I shall dine at Crib's tomorrow[1]. I like energy—even animal energy—of all kinds; and I have need of both mental and corporeal. I have not dined out, nor, indeed, *at all*, lately; have heard no music—have seen nobody. Now for a *plunge*—high life and low life. Amant *alterna* Camoenæ. (Journal, 23 Nov. 1813)

Other humorists may work more deeply in a more restricted field: Jonson among the gulls and tricksters of Jacobean London, Butler with the solemn lunacies of

---

[1] 'Gentleman' Jackson was Byron's boxing instructor. Tom Cribb (1781-1848) was one of the most famous professional pugilists of his day.

Caroline sectarians, Sheridan in the glittering world of the salons. Byron casts his net wider, if his fishing is more desultory than theirs. I shall continue, in the present section of this essay, to weave threads from his journals and critical writings in prose around the satiric centre in *English Bards*, returning to this centre to digest, as it were, what I have trapped. Byron touched life at many points. Admire as we may the more admirable of his contemporaries, the fact remains that Byron simply knew more about life—experienced more, and reflected on a wider range—than Wordsworth or Coleridge, than Shelley or Keats; and what he knew made him, not infrequently, smile where Wordsworth or Keats would have wept. In particular he had a deep conviction of the *limitations* of human knowledge and human powers, as against the 'human perfectibility' convictions of Shelley or Wordsworth's 'egotistical sublime'. His London life touched all strata of society, from peers to prostitutes, and on his travels abroad, as he notes in his journal, he is 'Today in a palace, tomorrow in a cow-house —this day with the Pacha, the next with a shepherd'.

It is precisely this sense of the complexity and limitations of human experience that establishes the tone for *English Bards and Scotch Reviewers*. The title itself is a kind of oxymoron. We expect a defence of the poets against their critics, but this is far from Byron's intent. He occupies a middle ground. The tone of maturity, of experience, is so firm that we find it hard to remember that this is technically a *juvenile* poem, written before the Eastern tour and the first years of fame. The poem opens with a Popean prologue on the prevalence of vice and its exposure by 'wit', followed by a disclaimer on Byron's part of any such high pretensions: his aim is simply to 'chase' literary 'follies':

> Laugh when I laugh, I seek no other fame;
> The cry is up, and scribblers are my game.   (43-4)

He himself has published 'A schoolboy freak, unworthy praise or blame'; it met with critical condemnation—but

with what title, Byron asks, do hacks like Jeffrey set themselves up as judges? The age itself is degenerate. 'Bards and
censors are so much alike' that there is little to choose between
them.

From this tentative opening Byron swings into a sustained
panegyric of the great Augustan age. A life-long admirer of
Pope, Byron did not share his fellow-Romantics' contempt
for eighteenth-century poetry.

> Time was, ere yet in these degenerate days
> Ignoble themes obtain'd mistaken praise,
> When sense and wit with poesy allied,
> No fabled graces, flourish'd side by side;
> From the same fount their inspiration drew,
> And, rear'd by taste, bloom'd fairer as they grew.
> Then, in this happy isle, a POPE's pure strain
> Sought the rapt soul to charm, nor sought in vain;
> A polish'd nation's praise aspired to claim,
> And raised the people's, as the poet's fame.
> Like him great DRYDEN pour'd the tide of song,
> In stream less smooth, indeed, yet doubly strong.
> Then CONGREVE's scenes could cheer, or OTWAY's
>   melt;
> For Nature then an English audience felt—
> But why these names, or greater still, retrace,
> When all to feebler bards resign their place?
> Yet to such times our lingering looks are cast,
> When taste and reason with those times are past. (103-20)

The standpoint is firmly neo-classical. Sense, Wit, Taste,
Reason, all the old counters devalued by Wordsworth and
Coleridge, are brought provocatively back into currency.
'Nature' is Pope's Nature, not Wordsworth's: the human
norm, the accepted world-picture, the congruence of what
is described with what is.

In what follows, Byron's scorn is directed against cant
and disproportion; in particular, against the inflation of
human potentialities. His standpoint is already that expressed
in his *Letter on . . . Bowles' Strictures on Pope*, written some
ten years later:

The truth is, that in these days the grand 'primum mobile' of England is *cant*; cant political, cant poetical, cant religious, cant moral; but always cant, multiplied through all the varieties of life. It is the fashion, and while it lasts will be too powerful for those who can only exist by taking the tone of the time. I say *cant*, because it is a thing of words, without the smallest influence upon human actions; the English being no wiser, no better, and much poorer, and divided among themselves, as well as far less moral, than they were before the prevalence of this verbal decorum.

The insight is prophetic as well as topical; cant, developed beyond Regency limits, was to be Britain's *primum mobile* for a century to come. This fact alone would account for Byron's down-grading by the Victorians. There were other considerations, of course, including Byron's scepticism about the inevitability of progress and the attainment of security. One of mankind's greatest 'idols' (in Bacon's sense of the word) is the thirst for permanence, and the compulsion to read permanence into a universe which is the theatre of incessant change.

. . . I do hate that word 'invariable'. What is there of *human*, be it poetry, philosophy, wit, wisdom, science, power, glory, mind, matter, life, or death, which is 'invariable'?

It is not simply Bowles that Byron is undermining here, but a whole human tendency: the bias towards disproportion, towards exaggeration and complacency.

Returning now to *English Bards*, we note that exaggeration, in its literary manifestations, works both ways—towards Grand Guignol on the one hand and silly sooth on the other. 'Tales of Terror jostle on the road' with 'strange, mysterious Dullness': Wordsworth's 'Idiot Boy' is an exaggeration, a departure from 'nature', as culpable in one direction as Mrs Radcliffe's Gothic horrors are in the other. In Scott's lays, 'mountain spirits prate to river sprites'; Southey's Thalaba, 'Arabia's monstrous, wild and wondrous son' overthrows 'More mad magicians than the world e'er knew' (143–56, 202–16). From inflated themes we pass to

inflated (or its opposite, sub-poetic) diction. Wordsworth is
concerned to show 'That prose is verse, and verse is merely
prose'; Coleridge, 'To turgid ode and tumid stanza dear',
substitutes obscurity for sublimity (235-64). It is penetrating,
entertaining, and just: Coleridge's early verses *are* tumid and
turgid, Wordsworth's rustic vignettes *are* obsessively
simpliste. But Byron knows where to stop. We find no
attacks on 'Tintern Abbey', no echoes of Southey's sneer at
The Ancient Mariner.

From lyrical and narrative poetry Byron turns to the
drama of his day, applying the same standards of proportion
and lucidity. Here we are even further removed from good
sense, from 'nature':

> Now to the Drama turn—Oh! motley sight!
> What precious scenes the wondering eyes invite:
> Puns, and a Prince within a barrel pent,
> And Dibdin's nonsense yield complete content.   (560-3)

In the rage for sensation, the boy-actor Master Betty—the
'infant Roscius'—has been hailed as a new Garrick. Nothing
survives of the stage once adorned by Shakespeare, Massin-
ger, Otway and Sheridan. The emphasis is on scenic display,
oblivious of the virtues of plot and characterization. Opera
has ousted tragedy and comedy alike.

> Then let Ausonia, skilled in every art
> To soften manners, but corrupt the heart,
> Pour her exotic follies o'er the town,
> To sanction Vice, and hunt Decorum down . . .
> Let high-born lechers eye the lively Presle
> Twirl her light limbs, that spurn the needless veil;
> Let Angiolini bare her breast of snow,
> Wave the white arm, and point the pliant toe . . .
> Whet not your scythe, Suppressors of our Vice!
> Reforming Saints! too delicately nice!
> By whose decrees, our sinful souls to save,
> No Sunday tankards foam, no barbers shave;
> And beer undrawn, and beards unmown, display
> Your holy reverence for the Sabbath-day.   (618-37)

The fun is irresistible; the vertiginous descent from the
opera-house to the yokels deprived by the Society for the
Suppression of Vice of their beer and Sunday shave establishes a new order of paradox, which Byron was to exploit
further in *Don Juan* (in which poem may also be found a
very similar and more devastating exposure of two-standard
morality in his appeal to Mrs Fry, X, lxxxv-lxxxvii).

So much for the 'bards', working in their main fields of
lyric, romance and drama. But what of the 'reviewers'?
Though we might expect Byron's main animus to be
directed here, we find him rapidly checked by the barren-
ness of his subject-matter. The poem actually begins with
an attack on the 'Scotch Reviewers'—but Byron knew very
little about them. And what he believed he knew was
mistaken. It had not been Jeffrey, but Brougham, who had
written the *Hours of Idleness* review. And of Jeffrey and his
character he has no personal knowledge. He can only play,
rather feebly, on the resemblance of his name to that of
the infamous 'hanging judge' of James II's day:

> Health to immortal JEFFREY! once, in name,
> England could boast a judge almost the same;
> In soul so like, so merciful, yet just,
> Some think that Satan has resigned his trust,
> And given the spirit to the world again,
> To sentence letters, as he sentenced men.   (438-43)

The tone is modulating here from sarcasm to irony, a much
keener weapon, and one which Byron is to use with some
skill in the middle and concluding sections of his poem. It
is the *Dunciad* which is now the Popean model, rather than
the *Moral Essays* or *An Essay in Criticism*; the details become
scurrilous and, as Byron admitted six years later, too personal.
One entry in his Journal for 1816 reads: 'Too ferocious—
this is mere insanity'; and many more express regret at
having written the satire at all. But Byron did not reach his
full command of irony until thirteen years later, in *The
Vision of Judgment*. In that poem he was to have the target,
Southey, well between his sights. The contemptuous

geniality with which he disposes of the Laureate is much more devastating than the Dunciadic scurrility of his onslaught on Jeffrey.

Even in writing his first and most spleenful satire Byron could not be less than himself, a poet of Shakespearian diversity of tone. All is not invective and denigration. There are tributes to 'neglected genius', to Burns, Campbell, Crabbe, Cowper. Beside the humour and even farce of his comments on minor poets (their names forgotten today) we have the elegiac tenderness of the lines on his Cambridge contemporary, Henry Kirke White (831–48), which may have contributed a resonance to *Adonais*, the elevation of the paragraph on Wright's *Horæ Ionicæ* (867–80), where Canto II of *Childe Harold* is anticipated ('Where Attic flowers Aonian odours breathe' 884), and the moral indignation of those sections of the poem which deal with the opera, the dance and the gaming-house.

The closing paragraphs of *English Bards* are already modulating from the English scene to the Mediterranean:

> Yet once again, adieu! ere this the sail
> That wafts me hence is shivering in the gale;
> And Afric's coast and Calpe's adverse height,
> And Stamboul's minarets must greet my sight ...   (1017–20)

and Byron's next satires, *Hints from Horace* and *The Curse of Minerva*, were to be composed 'Where Attic flowers Aonian odours breathe'. He is now in his right setting and there is a sense of relaxation, of poise, of urbanity. We have left the glooms and grumpiness of Newstead, Cambridge, London. In bright air, Byron can write airily and dismissively of

> The groves of Granta, and her gothic halls,
> King's Coll., Cam's stream, stain'd windows, and old walls,
>   (H.H.27–8)

and patronizingly of Jeffrey:

> Again, my Jeffrey!—as that sound inspires,
> How wakes my bosom to its wonted fires!
> Fires, such as gentle Caledonians feel
> When Southrons writhe upon their critic wheel . . .   (589–92)

And though he recurs to his old *Hours of Idleness* grievance, and even threatens the 'Dear damned contemner of [his] schoolboy songs' with his 'hate', he wryly confesses himself baffled by Jeffrey's bland omission to react to *English Bards and Scotch Reviewers* (599–626).[1]

Hints from Horace is then, in some sense, a continuation of the earlier satire. The old themes are taken up—fury at the reception of *Hours of Idleness*, dislike of the Lake School of poets (and we note that Southey is becoming the main target of attack, in lines 653–62), support for neo-classical standards. But the bulk of the poem is occupied with technical points—with judgements on what kind of form is suitable for what kind of subject, on the relative merits of blank verse and couplets, and so on. It is, in fact, a 'Poetics', or 'Essay in Criticism', based on Horace's Epistle 'Ad Pisones', or 'De Arte Poetica', and the original Latin text is run along at the bottom of each page so that the reader may judge how well Byron is doing his job of adapting his classical model to Regency conditions. 'Imitations of Horace', or of Juvenal, had been a favourite form in the preceding age: Pope gives us one example, Dr Johnson another. For Byron, plainly, the challenge to his virtuosity was attractive, and he does produce a satire *sui generis* which yet sticks pretty closely to its original. Written in 1811, during his Athenian sojourn, *Hints from Horace* is a kind of æsthetic stocktaking, a summing-up of his criteria and allegiances. Decorum is firmly stressed, as was 'Nature' in *English Bards*.

> The greater portion of the rhyming tribe
> (Give ear, my friend, for thou hast been a scribe)
> Are led astray by some peculiar lure.
> I labour to be brief—become obscure;

[1] Unwhipped, the top ceases to spin!

> One falls while following elegance too fast;
> Another soars, inflated with bombast: . . .
> New words find credit in these latter days
> If neatly grafted on a Gallic phrase.
> What Chaucer, Spenser did, we scarce refuse
> To Dryden's or to Pope's maturer muse.
> If you can add a little, say why not,
> As well as William Pitt, and Walter Scott?
> Since they, by force of rhyme and force of lungs,
> Enrich'd our island's ill-united tongues . . .   (39–86)

It is judicious, neatly turned, relaxed, without the coiled-spring tension of *English Bards*. There is nothing original in the praise of decorum. Yet Byron does not leave the matter there. He goes a step beyond the standpoint of the earlier satire. Even 'correctness' must give way to the 'glowing thoughts' of genius:

> And must the bard his glowing thoughts confine,
> Lest censure hover o'er some faulty line?
> Remove whate'er a critic may suspect,
> To gain the paltry suffrage of '*correct*'?
> Or prune the spirit of each daring phrase,
> To fly from error, not to merit praise?   (417–22)

It would be futile to maintain that *Hints from Horace* is a work with much attraction for the modern reader; that is perhaps less its fault than ours. But to read it is to gain an expansion of one's knowledge of Byron's mind, and to correct the settled prejudice that he was not a very serious literary practitioner. His next satire, *The Curse of Minerva*, may be more congenial because more dramatic and more rooted in the Greek scene. Its stage is the Parthenon, its actors Athena, Byron, Elgin, its time-scheme in one sense a single evening and in another sense the whole of history. Technically, the unities are preserved; psychologically, we are in a world of multiple dimensions. To count it a literary satire we have to give 'literary' a rather wide sense; perhaps 'cultural' would be better, or even 'ethnic'. 'Satire' too might well be replaced by 'polemic' or 'diatribe'.

To understand what sort of a poem *The Curse of Minerva* is we have to remember Byron's curious gift for falling in love with a place as easily as with a person, and perhaps more easily; and I am not using 'fall in love' figuratively. We have to remember the tenderness of 'How Venice once was dear' in *Childe Harold* IV, iii, the old attachment to Harrow, the indignation at the suggestion that Troy was a myth. Athens too had now (1811) been taken under Byron's wing. He felt keenly the depredations practised on her yet remaining glories by such antiquaries as Lord Elgin. *Quod non fecerunt Goti, hoc fecerunt Scoti*[1], were the words 'very deeply cut', as Hobhouse reports, in the plaster wall which filled the gap left by Elgin. In his confrontation with Athena on the floor of the ruined Parthenon Byron makes an important point (125–56) of the fact that her 'plunderer' is a Scot, not an Englishman. Britannia's honour is thus, to some extent, saved.

Perhaps I might at this point try to correct a misconception about Byron's attitude to 'antiquities'—a misconception current since Lady Blessington reported that 'antiquities had no interest for him', and repeated *ad nauseam* up to the present day. It is true that Byron had no love for antiquities as antiquities, as relics of the past torn from their context and mummified in museums and galleries. But he did care enormously, passionately, for 'antiquities' as 'eternities', if I may so put it, as manifestations of the living past which itself is an aspect of the eternal moment through which man lives and is lived. In the extant evidences of the ancient world, through which that world still, in a way, breathes and comforts and reproaches modern man—in this he *was* interested (if one can apply so feeble a word to Byron's total commitment). The commitment was more than a speculative one: as I have suggested in the first of these essays, it was Byron's unique task to make himself a vehicle of reintegration of past and present, of revitalization of a space-time continuum covering the Mediterranean world.

1 What the Goths had spared, the Scots destroyed.

And this task he undertook in a series of atoning *gestures* leading up to the final sacrificial act. One minor gesture among many which has been totally misunderstood is his swim from Sestos to Abydos. To his biographers and commentators this is a feat of physical skill of which Byron was childishly proud and to which he referred too often; but for Byron himself it was a work of historical salvage, a re-insertion through living action of a portion of the past into the present, an act of piety, a triumph over time. 'Actions are our epochs', as he succinctly puts it in *Manfred*.[1]

It is an index of the extraordinary *continuity* of Byron's mind (through all its surface fluctuations and inconsistencies) that *The Curse of Minerva* develops a theme already adumbrated in *English Bards and Scotch Reviewers*, 1027–32:

> Let ABERDEEN and ELGIN still pursue
> The shade of fame through regions of Virtù . . .
> And make their grand saloons a general mart
> For all the mutilated blocks of art . . .

But now, in 1811, he is on the spot, standing within the temple these 'Scoti' have desecrated:

> As thus, within the walls of Pallas' fane,
> I mark'd the beauties of the land and main,
> Alone, and friendless, on the magic shore,
> Whose arts and arms but live in poets' lore,
> Oft as the matchless dome I turn'd to scan,
> Sacred to gods, but not secure from man,
> The past return'd, the present seem'd to cease,
> And Glory knew no clime beyond her Greece! (55–62)

It is from such a rooting in a here-and-now that stretches out to historical and mythological vistas that Byron's

---

[1] If I am right about this, we can see a deeper significance than the coincidental in his remark to Shelley 'that our danger from the storm took place precisely in the spot where Julie and her lover [in Rousseau's *La Nouvelle Héloise*] were nearly overset . . .' (Shelley, Letter to Peacock of 12 July 1816).

imagination always draws its best sustenance. Conditions
are ideal for the creation of a great poem. And a great poem
The Curse of Minerva undoubtedly is. One wonders why its
importance has been so assiduously soft-pedalled.

The work opens with Byron's most glowing couplets.

> Slow sinks, more lovely ere his race be run,
> Along Morea's hills the setting sun;
> Not, as in northern climes, obscurely bright,
> But one unclouded blaze of living light . . .

This whole passage, down to line 54, is a brilliant land-and-
seascape diptych exhibited first in the light of the setting
sun and then under the full moon. It was transferred bodily
to the opening of the third canto of *The Corsair* when
Byron, for various reasons, abandoned any idea of publishing
The Curse. In an earlier essay[1] I have suggested that it 'fits
much better there'; this is a judgement I should now like to
recant. It does fit beautifully into the Tale, but the Tale
could do without it. Not so the satire; it is an essential note
in its counterpoint. For it is only in the context of light and
space, island and promontory, sea and mountain, that Byron's
impassioned plea receives its full meaning. Note—and this is
crucial to Byron's stance—that there is no antiquarianism, no
Hellenic purism. The Parthenon projects the total history of
Greece, which includes the Turkish occupation as well as
the classical past.[2] Byron reminds us, subtly, that under the
moon which is Islam's symbol as well as Diana's, the mosque
as well as the temple is 'sacred', and that the olive is a holy
tree for the Koran[3] as for the cult of Pallas.

> But lo! from high Hymettus to the plain
> The queen of night asserts her silent reign;
> No murky vapour, herald of the storm,
> Hides her fair face, or girds her glowing form.

[1] See *Byron I: Lyric and Romance*, p. 45.

[2] 'Dome' in line 59 is a catchword for 'massive structure', but the
Parthenon of 1811 actually included a post-classical dome.

[3] Cf. the 'blessed olive tree, neither eastern nor western', of the Koran,
sura 24.

> With cornice glittering as the moon beams play,
> There the white column greets her grateful ray,
> And bright around, with quivering gleams beset,
> Her emblem sparkles o'er the minaret:
> The groves of olive scatter'd dark and wide,
> Where meek Cephisus sheds his scanty tide,
> The cypress saddening by the sacred mosque,
> The gleaming turret of the gay kiosk,
> And sad and sombre mid the holy calm,
> Near Theseus' fane, yon solitary palm . . .   (33–46)

Here is Byron's inclusive vision, couched in a medium brilliantly adapted to its complexities. This is the Popean regular couplet: no enjambements, no metrical looseness. Yet Byron makes it *dance*—and of course it dances *because* it keeps to the pattern, with subtle variations of rhythm insufficient to disturb the basic design.[1] The dance here is an intellectual, one might almost say a metaphysical thing: a dance of contrasts, of cultures and emblems of cultures, the interweaving of domes and minarets with columns and cornices, a marriage of atoning gestures. Sad cypress (already noted by Byron for its presence in Moslem graveyards) raises its sword above the thalassic flow of fruitful olive groves. And it is into this ethnic symbiosis, this delicate balance of cultures, that Elgin so crassly intrudes.

Among all the other things we can identify *The Curse of Minerva* as being—satire, description, polemic, apology, prophecy—it is worth noting that it is also an example of that ancient form the 'vision': a 'kind' dear to the Middle Ages and popular right up to our own day. As Byron muses within the desecrated temple, Pallas herself appears to him—majestic, but no longer the awesome power of old time:

> . . . though still the brightest of the sky,
> Celestial tears bedimm'd her large blue eye;

[1] For the kind of couplet which cannot dance because it is too dissolute, too far emancipated from its frame, the reader may compare Keats's *Endymion*. For a couplet like Byron's, but used for quite other purposes, he might look at lines 47–90 of *The Rape of the Lock*.

Round the rent casque her owlet circled slow,
And mourn'd his mistress with a shriek of woe!   (85-8)

(How Byronic that owlet!—for the ancients a stereotype of
wisdom, but here rescued from the abstract and made into
something living and feeling, sharing its mistress's sorrows
as might a faithful dog or horse.) The situation closely
resembles that at the opening of *Childe Harold* II,[1] but now
it is 'august Athena' herself who speaks, delivering a sustained invective on Lord Elgin which occupies the rest of
the poem.[2] First tracing the fortunes of the 'relics torn that
yet remain' in the Acropolis—

> *These* Cecrops placed, *this* Pericles adorn'd,
> *That* Adrian rear'd when drooping Science mourn'd—
>
> (101-2)

relics which have ''scaped from the ravage of the Turk and
Goth', she pours savage scorn on their latest plunderer:

> So when the lion quits his fell repast,
> Next prowls the wolf, the filthy jackal last . . .   (113-14)

Then comes the curse itself: a retraction of 'her counsels'
(i.e. of wisdom) from the land that gave Elgin birth, and the
subsequent train of evils moral, political and cultural.
The presence of the marbles in London will prove the
degradation of art, not its salvation. Here Byron's satire is
at its naughtiest:

> Round the throng'd gate shall sauntering coxcombs creep,
> To lounge and lucubrate, to prate and peep;
> While many a languid maid, with longing sigh,
> On giant statues casts the curious eye;
> The room with transient glance appears to skim,
> Yet marks the mighty back and length of limb;
> Mourns o'er the difference of *now* and *then;*
> Exclaims, 'These Greeks indeed were proper men!' . . .
>
> (183-90)

[1] See *Byron I: Lyric and Romance*, p. 20.
[2] Apart from the poet's intervention to protest that Elgin was not an
Englishman, already noted.

Next the canker of corruption, of perfidy, implicit in
Elgin's criminal deed, will spread to every aspect of English
life. Her allies will fall away from her; her empire will decay:

> Look to the East, where Ganges' swarthy race
> Shall shake your tyrant empire to its base . . .   (221-2)

The final defeat will come with the moral and economic
collapse of Britain herself:

> Look last at home—ye love not to look there;
> On the grim smile of comfortless despair:
> Your city saddens: loud though Revel howls,
> Here Famine faints, and yonder Rapine prowls . . .
>
> Now fare ye well! enjoy your little hour;
> Go, grasp the shadow of your vanish'd power;
> Gloss o'er the failure of each fondest scheme;
> Your strength a name, your bloated wealth a dream . . .
>
> (239-42; 259-62)

We are again in the presence of the prophetic Byron, with
a statesman's eye for cause and effect, the Byron who in
the House of Lords opposed the death penalty for the
Nottingham frame-breakers, and pilloried the Act of
Union between England and Ireland as the act of union
'between the shark and its prey'. And again we may guess
how such predictions would appear to his own age of
colonial and commercial expansion. We have less excuse,
today, for disregarding *The Curse of Minerva*.

III. *HEBREW MELODIES*
AND TRANSITIONAL LYRICS

The two groups of poems I shall now discuss might have
been entitled 'Poems of Attachment and Separation', for
while perhaps none of them is actually addressed to Annabella Milbanke, they are largely concerned with an idealized
image of womanhood: a being virginal yet maternal,

protective yet remote.[1] So remote, indeed, that like
Wordsworth's Lucy she passes outside the human context to
inhabit a world of tides and starry spaces and elemental
dance.

Hebrew Melodies (1815) is a collection of songs mainly
with a Biblical background which served a typically
Byronic double purpose: to make money to help pay off
his creditors and to assist a Jewish composer, Isaac Nathan,
who wanted lyrics for his accompaniments of '*real old
indisputed Hebrew melodies*, which are beautiful and to which
David & the prophets actually sang the "Songs of Zion"—
& I have done nine or ten on the sacred model . . .' (Letter
of 20 Oct. 1814 to Annabella Milbanke.) Again we note
Byron's lasting interest in the Bible and in traditional tunes,
ballads and legends,[2] the folk-song which had cheered the
Prisoner of Chillon in his captivity and which is to captivate
the exiled mutineers of *The Island*. The collection opens
with 'She Walks in Beauty, like the Night', a lyric which
has no biblical background, and which I shall discuss later;
then swings into what can best be described as a short ode on
King David and the power of music. This Augustan theme
is resumed and amplified in two further lyrics, 'Saul' and
'The Song of Saul before His Last Battle'. The first of these
is a thrilling evocation of the Witch of Endor's raising of
the ghost of the prophet Samuel at Saul's command:

> Thou whose spell can raise the dead,
>> Bid the prophet's form appear.
>> 'Samuel, raise thy buried head!
>> King, behold the phantom seer!'
> Earth yawn'd; he stood the centre of a cloud:

[1] It is worth noting the frequent references to the Virgin Mary in *Don
Juan*, and his 'adoring', almost obsessive love for first Mary Duff and later
Mary Chaworth. He is careful to inform us, in 'Elegy on Newstead Abbey',
that the abbey is dedicated to the Virgin. 'I have a passion for the name of
Mary', he confesses in *Don Juan*, V, iv.

[2] Ossian was an early favourite, imitated in 'The Death of Calmar and
Orla' (*Hours of Idleness*): 'Past is the race of heroes! but their fame rises on
the harp; their souls ride on the wings of the wind!'

Light changed its hue, retiring from his shroud.
Death stood all glassy in his fixed eye;
His hand was wither'd, and his veins were dry;
His foot, in bony whiteness, glitter'd there,
Shrunken, and sinewless, and ghastly bare;
From lips that moved not and unbreathing frame,
Like cavern'd winds, the hollow accents came.
Saul saw, and fell to earth, as falls the oak,
At once, and blasted by the thunder-stroke ...   (1-14)

The power of stark visualization here surpasses most things
in his earlier writing.

The same dramatic instancy is heard again in 'The
Destruction of Sennacherib' and 'The Vision of Belshazzar'.
The first of these is too well-known to need comment here;
the second achieves a bare-bone intensity hardly to be met
with again before Hardy and Housman:

> In that same hour and hall,
>   The fingers of a hand
> Came forth against the wall,
>   And wrote as if on sand:
> The fingers of a man—
>   A solitary hand
> Along the letters ran
>   And traced them like a wand.   (ii)

The implicated repetition emphasizes the eeriness of the
occurrence. And the last poem in the collection, a para-
phrase from the Book of Job, plays on the same super-
natural nerve.

These are what Blake would have called (*Jerusalem*, 'To
the Reader') 'the terrific numbers' and they are largely
concerned with war, with power and with the occult.
The 'mild & gentle' lyrics express more personal themes,
often touching on the mystery of death: 'If that High
World', 'My Soul is Dark', 'Oh! Snatch'd Away in Beauty's
Bloom', 'I saw Thee Weep', 'Sun of the Sleepless!', 'When
Coldness Wraps This Suffering Clay'; while others take up
the theme of exile: 'On Jordan's Banks', 'The Wild Gazelle',

'O Weep for Those', 'By the Rivers of Babylon', 'On the Day of the Destruction of Jerusalem by Titus'; or of less public grief in 'Jephtha's Daughter' and 'Herod's Lament for Mariamne'. There is an extraordinary richness of topics and rhythms, clearly preluding the great music which was to come in *The Siege of Corinth* and *Manfred*. For sheer lyrical grace Byron never surpassed his achievement in 'Oh! Snatch'd Away in Beauty's Bloom', a lament for which the model is plainly Collins but which transcends the simple pathos of 'How Sleep the Brave!'

> Oh! snatch'd away in beauty's bloom,
> On thee shall press no ponderous tomb;
>> But on thy turf shall roses rear
>> Their leaves, the earliest of the year;
> And the wild cypress wave in tender gloom . . .

Byron's effects, here and in the two remaining stanzas, are gained by extremely subtle metrical shifts; the interlacing rhythms follow the fluctuations of emotion, generating in cross-currents of the two couplets a tension which is released in the lengthened fifth line. Note too how the antithetic imagery contributes its *structural* counterpoint: the evanescence of 'snatch'd away' is balanced by the ponderous pressure of the second line, 'bloom' by 'tomb'; soaring images reassert themselves with 'turf', 'roses rear their leaves'. The final exotic 'cypress' adds a touch of mystery, lifts the poem out of the English scene into an imaginative landscape. In the second stanza—

> And oft by yon blue gushing stream
> Shall Sorrow lean her drooping head . . .

—it would be easy to demonstrate the superiority of Byron's single Personification to Collins's collection (Fancy, Honour, Freedom) by pointing out the work it has to do, and does. The earlier Romantics—Wordsworth, Coleridge—had begun by outlawing the Personification, but it forced its way back into currency to fill a need their own practice engendered. It returned enriched and revitalized. Shelley's

'Eternal Hunger' in *Adonais*, Byron's 'Sorrow' here, and indeed Wordsworth's own 'Fear and trembling Hope, Silence and Foresight' in 'Yew-trees', are potent beyond the mode of Thomson or Collins.

The more powerful the mind, the more liable it is to explosions from the dynamic centre; the more subtle it is, the more vulnerable to disturbances of balance and harmony. Byron's mind was both subtle and powerful, but it lacked a steadying influence. What wonder if in Annabella (who copied the *Melodies* out for him) he imagined he had found one? Mixed with the exilic and martial songs of the *Melodies* we note these more nostalgic strains: the theme of the faultless, remotely perfect woman ('She walks in beauty'), the Iphigenia ('Jephtha's Daughter'), the *ewig weibliche* moving between smiles and tears ('I saw thee weep'). These are ideal projections upon an as yet little known Annabella. If in the end she did not come up to that ideal figure, the blame hardly rests with Annabella. But in his famous (or notorious) 'Fare Thee Well! and if for ever . . .' (17 March 1816) Byron was saying goodbye not merely to Annabella but to any hope of an Iphigenia figure in his life. His despair and resentment for this were expressed, unworthily, in the even more notorious 'A Sketch' which pours bitter scorn on the lady's maid, Mrs Clermont, whom he suspected of poisoning his wife's mind against him. Neither of these poems, though they made much stir at the time, merits our attention as poetry.

From Annabella Byron's emotional revulsion was to an earlier Iphigenia figure, his half-sister Augusta. The Augusta-Byron relationship and the Dorothy-Wordsworth one are oddly similar, even down to the hints of incest— itself a major Romantic theme. This is the 'all nameless' guilt which is the mainspring of *Manfred*, but in these transitional lyrics we hear only of the Egeria side of the relationship, the tenderness and understanding that led Wordsworth to write his 'She gave me eyes, she gave me ears', and Byron his 'Stanzas to Augusta':

> When fortune changed—and love fled far,
>   And hatred's shafts flew thick and fast,
> Thou wert the solitary star
>   Which rose and set not to the last . . .   (iii)
>
> Thou stood'st, as stands a lovely tree,
>   That still unbroke, though gently bent,
> Still waves with fond fidelity
>   Its boughs above a monument . . .   (vii)

We are still in the world of 'Oh! Snatch'd Away . . .!'
The second set of 'Stanzas to Augusta' is less successful:
jaunty anapæsts hardly fit this theme; but the 'Epistle to
Augusta', written in 1816 (Byron is by now on the Continent), but not published until six years after the poet's death,
reinforces the love-childhood-nature motif:

> I feel almost at times as I have felt
> In happy childhood; trees, and flowers, and brooks,
> Which do remember me of where I dwelt
> Ere my young mind was sacrificed to books,
> Come as of yore upon me, and can melt
> My heart with recognition of their looks;
> And even at moments I could think I see
> Some living thing to love—but none like thee.   (vii)

We are witnessing a revulsion and a regression; from the
disappointment of his marriage back to Augusta, back to
childhood, to Scotland, even to the dark watershed of the
streams of birth and death:

> Could I remount the river of my years
> To the first fountain of our smiles and tears,
> I would not trace again the stream of hours
> Between their outworn banks of wither'd flowers,
> But bid it flow as now—until it glides
> Into the number of the nameless tides . . .

These lines open a 'fragment' (Diodati, July 1816) which we
may regret Byron's failure to complete, since it is of an
intensity rarely met with in reflective verse and it begins to
touch on themes—the meaning of Death, the identity of

absence with death, the possibility that the dead enjoy some
kind of shadowy consciousness:

> ... do they in their silent cities dwell
> Each in his incommunicative cell?
> Or have they their own language? and a sense
> Of breathless being?—darken'd and intense
> As midnight in her solitude? ...

on which we would gladly hear Byron further. But of
course these were to be the themes of *Manfred* and of the
group of reflective poems we have now to consider.

IV. REFLECTIVE LYRICS AND LONGER POEMS

> ... To keep the mind
> Deep in its fountain ...

This intense aspiration, first voiced in *Childe Harold* (III,
lxix), lies at the core of Byron's reflective—or, as it might
better be called, intuitive—verse. For Byron is not a poet of
reflection as is Wordsworth, Coleridge or even Keats.
T. S. Eliot, in a famous passage of criticism, talked of the
Romantics 'ruminating'. Byron does not ruminate, chew
the cud of recollected experience, nor does he ratiocinate,
building systems on glimpses of 'reality' or 'truth'. I have
written in an earlier essay of Byron's capacity for reacting
with his whole being to an immediate experience; there was
thus no 'space' left over for him, as it were, to dwell upon
memory-data, he is too busy with the here-and-now, and
the intersection of the here-and-now not with the stream of
recollection but with the shaft of eternity. Byron's problem
is the complexity and insistence of sense-data; he recognizes
in himself the danger of being submerged and carried away
by the torrent of events, and his 'reflective' poetry focuses
a constant effort to anchor himself in the inner source of his
being. Those who knew him in his early years, or accom-
panied him on his travels, remark again and again on his

habit of withdrawing suddenly and unexpectedly from 'the hot throng' to sit alone for hour upon hour on some rock overlooking the sea, plunged deep in the exploratory and revitalizing contact with his innermost self.[1] The same note often sounds in the private Journals, though tinged even here with the mocking self-depreciation which runs through his letters and reported conversation:

I do not know that I am happiest when alone; but this I am sure of, that I never am long in the society even of *her* I love, (God knows too well, and the devil probably too,) without a yearning for the company of my lamp and my utterly confused and tumbled-over library . . . I have sparred for exercise (windows open) with Jackson an hour daily, to attenuate and keep up the ethereal part of me. The more violent the fatigue, the better my spirits for the rest of the day; and then, my evenings have that calm nothingness of languor, which I most delight in . . . (10 April 1814).

This 'calm nothingness of languor' is very close to Words-worth's 'wise passiveness' and even closer to the Keatsian 'indolence' on which I have commented at length in my book *The Consecrated Urn;* what I have had to say there (especially on pp. 56–66) may very largely be applied to Byron too. But we must be careful to distinguish Keats's 'indolence' from his 'speculation' or reflection.

A similar division to 'indolence'/'speculation' may be of use in categorizing Byron's later lyrics: we might see it as 'calm nothingness of languor'/'metaphysics' (one of Byron's favourite words, as his letters and journals show). The mood of 'all passion spent' suffuses the lyrics of the first category. 'All things remount to a fountain, though they may flow to an ocean', he remarks in his 'Detached Thoughts' (No. 101), thus neatly summing up the inner and outward movements of his thought which I dwelt upon in an earlier essay. If this final sentence of Thought 101 represents his

[1] 'They show a tomb in the churchyard at Harrow, commanding a view over Windsor, which was so well known to be his favourite resting-place, that the boys called it "Byron's Tomb"; and here, they say, he used to sit for hours, wrapt up in thought.' (*Works of Byron*, 1832, Vol. VII, p. 49, footnote.)

'calm nothingness' side, the 'speculation' with which the Thought opens: '... I sometimes think that *Man* may be the relic of some higher material being, wrecked in a former world, and degenerated in the hardships and struggle through Chaos into Conformity . . . as the Elements become more inexorable . . .' belongs to his 'metaphysical' thinking: such a retraction from the cosmic to 'the mind deep in its fountain' is characteristic of Byron. Speculations on the origin, nature, and destiny of Man are of course important factors in his Biblical dramas (which will be discussed in my third essay) but they also motivate a number of non-dramatic and non-lyrical poems. Of these 'Darkness' is the best-known example.

This poem, one of Byron's very rare excursions into blank verse outside the dramas, was originally called 'A Dream'. It was written during Byron's residence at Geneva, and is dated July 1816. Jeffrey's comment will serve both as a summary and as an indication of how it was received by contemporary opinion:

'Darkness' is a grand and gloomy sketch of the supposed consequences of the final extinction of the Sun and the heavenly bodies; executed, undoubtedly, with great and fearful force, but with something of German exaggeration, and a fantastical solution of incidents. The very conception is terrible above all conception of known calamity, and is too oppressive to the imagination to be contemplated with pleasure, even in the faint reflection of poetry.

Sir Walter Scott, usually one of Byron's most appreciative critics, found the poem obscure and 'feverish'. 'The waste of boundless space into which they lead the poet, the neglect of precision which such themes may render habitual, make them, in respect to poetry, what mysticism is to religion'. But in fact there is nothing obscure or feverish about the poem itself. It is a fragment of science fiction in verse (the theme of The Last Man was interesting many writers at this time) written with an almost clinical precision of statement which makes the horror of the subject even more intense.

It is interesting to remember that *The Ancient Mariner* too had been greeted (by Southey) as 'a Dutch attempt at German sublimity'. The opening lines of 'Darkness' give the gist of the theme:

> I had a dream, which was not all a dream.
> The bright sun was extinguish'd, and the stars
> Did wander darkling in the eternal space,
> Rayless, and pathless, and the icy earth
> Swung blind and blackening in the moonless air;
> Morn came and went—and came, and brought no day,
> And men forgot their passions in the dread
> Of this their desolation; and all hearts
> Were chill'd into a selfish prayer for light:
> And they did live by watch-fires—and the thrones,
> The palaces of crowned kings—the huts,
> The habitations of all things which dwell,
> Were burnt for beacons . . .

The writing is notably firm and controlled. There is no plot, and little emotional development, though the fidelity of a dog guarding the corpse of its master provides a moment of Byronic pathos.

Also dated July 1816 is another blank verse poem, 'The Dream', which is a mournful celebration of his love for Mary Chaworth and at the same time a sort of emotional 'Tintern Abbey', presenting Byron's inner progress from warm idealism to desolation and despair. This is a longer and more personally interesting poem than 'Darkness', and deserves fuller comment than I can give it here. The opening section explores one of Byron's deepest preoccupations, the relationship between sleeping and waking, and of both with the creative act. Note the greater lightness and flexibility of the verse; this is Byron's speaking voice:

> Our life is twofold: Sleep hath its own world,
> A boundary between the things misnamed
> Death and existence: Sleep hath its own world,
> And a wide realm of wild reality . . .   (1-4)

The nature of dreams is discussed:

> . . . they speak
> Like sibyls, of the future; they have power—
> The tyranny of pleasure and of pain;
> They make us what we were not—what they will,
> And shake us with the vision that's gone by,
> The dread of vanish'd shadows . . .   (11-17)

One such dream occupies the remainder of the poem. In section ii the mournful confessional music begins:

> I saw two beings in the hues of youth
> Standing upon a hill, a gentle hill,
> Green and of mild declivity . . .
>   the hill
> Was crown'd with a peculiar diadem
> Of trees, in circular array, so fix'd,
> Not by the sport of nature, but of man . . .
> The maid was on the eve of womanhood;
> The boy had fewer summers, but his heart
> Had far outgrown his years, and to his eye
> There was but one beloved face on earth,
> And that was shining on him . . .

Here, plainly, we have a further regression from the mortifying fiasco of his marriage—beyond Augusta, now, to boyhood dreams and hopes; but they too had issued in frustration and humiliation. 'Do you think I could care anything for that lame boy?', Mary Chaworth is reported to have remarked to her maid; and Byron overheard her, or was told of the remark. No wonder his first title for 'The Dream' was 'The Destiny', Byron's lifelong destiny of frustration, from the initial lameness right up to the final tragi-comedy of Missolonghi.

> Time taught him a deep answer—when she loved
> Another; even *now* she loved another,
> And on the summit of that hill she stood
> Looking afar if yet her lover's steed
> Kept pace with her expectancy, and flew.   (ii. 70-4)

Byron never wrote better blank verse than this; the last two lines have a Dantesque bareness and shudder.

The remaining seven short sections trace Byron's life in its stages as an emotional drama rooted in this primal trauma: an Oresteia, as it were, reduced from dynastic to personal terms. Section iv shows him 'a wanderer' in 'the wilds/Of fiery climes . . ./And his Soul drank their sunbeams':

> —— and in the last he lay . . .
> Couch'd among fallen columns, in the shade
> Of ruin'd walls that had survived the names
> Of those who rear'd them . . .

In section vi his marriage is briefly touched upon:

> The Wanderer was return'd.—I saw him stand
> Before an Altar—with a gentle bride;
> Her face was fair, but was not that which made
> The Starlight of his Boyhood . . .

In section viii he is 'alone as heretofore':

> The beings which surrounded him were gone,
> Or were at war with him; he was a mark
> For blight and desolation, compass'd round
> With Hatred and Contention; Pain was mix'd
> In all which was served up to him, until,
> Like to the Pontic monarch of old days,
> He fed on poisons, and they had no power,
> But were a kind of nutriment; he lived
> Through that which had been death to many men,
> And made him friends of mountains: with the stars
> And the quick Spirit of the Universe
> He held his dialogues; and they did teach
> To him the magic of their mysteries;
> To him the book of Night was open'd wide,
> And voices from the deep abyss reveal'd
> A marvel and a secret—— Be it so.

Already, here, is emerging the figure of the Magus, the wizard endowed through guilt and suffering with powers to probe the secrets of the universe, 'the book of Night', the Anima Mundi, who is to dominate *Manfred* and the other metaphysical dramas. But this is a theme for my third essay.

In my first essay I presented Byron as a vortex moving through a space-time continuum, encountering historical vortices, reactivating and being reactivated by them. The ideogram of the vortical hero is fully present in the Ossianic imitation of *Hours of Idleness*, 'The Death of Calmar and Orla':

He looks down from eddying tempests: he rolls his form in the whirl-wind, and hovers on the blast of the mountain . . . his yellow locks . . . streamed like the meteor of the night . . .

and persists through the varied fortunes of *Childe Harold* and the Oriental Tales. But lacking external stimulus the vortex comes, from time to time, to a standstill. The lyrics and longer poems we have just studied belong to one of these periods of calm which so rapidly degenerate into stretches of stagnation. Escaping to the Continent, Byron was able once more to expose himself to the stimuli radiating from time-place nuclei which vibrated on his wave-length, as well as to exciting human contacts both sexual and intellectual.

The renewal is at once apparent in *Manfred* and the last two Cantos of *Childe Harold*, and in a handful of shorter poems as well. Of these by far the most important is the Venice poem, 'So We'll Go No More A Roving', which achieves a poised synthesis of rest and motion. Before considering it in detail I should like to glance back at two well-known songs belonging to the transitional period: 'She Walks in Beauty', which opens the *Hebrew Melodies*, and 'Stanzas for Music', both of which belong to the same dialectical order. We have already noted how in 'Oh! Snatch'd Away In Beauty's Bloom' Byron's personal vortex is brought to rest on the antithesis of death: bloom/tomb, early roses/wild cypress—to be set spinning again under the torsion of these very antitheses:

> Away! we know that tears are vain,
> That Death nor hears nor heeds distress . . .

In 'She Walks in Beauty' the opening antithesis, beauty/
night, is developed through the first stanza: cloudless climes/
starry sky, dark and bright, tender light/gaudy day, purely
physical contrasts which the second stanza transmutes
into terms of art:

> One shade the more, one ray the less,
>   Had half impair'd the nameless grace
> Which waves in every raven tress,
>   Or softly lightens o'er her face;
> Where thoughts serenely sweet express
>   How pure, how dear their dwelling-place.

And already, with the last two lines, we are passing into the
lyric's third dimension of character and so into the world of
the third stanza.

This poem has no real connexion with the rest of the
Hebrew Melodies, but was written down by Byron on his
return from a ball where he had seen for the first time 'his
cousin, the beautiful Mrs Wilmot who had appeared in
mourning with numerous spangles on her dress'. Thus the
poem has its link with death, though death is nowhere
mentioned in the poem, and we can grasp the situational
antitheses, the whirl of the dance, 'the hot throng', the still
centre of the woman appreciated as an icon of remote,
unapproachable beauty, the starry-spangled robe. The
pronoun 'I' is absent from this as from the other three poems
of this group; and if we should find ourselves comparing
'She Walks in Beauty' with Wordsworth's 'She Was a
Phantom of Delight' (a tempting exercise) I suppose this
lack of the personal, of the possessive, in Byron's poem is
the first point we should make.

Here we are at the Byronic centre. Under the æsthetic
shock of the woman's appearance in such a gathering the
vortex begins to spin, but gently, with no generation of
heat. 'There be None of Beauty's Daughters' (27 March

1815) is in a sense even more central. The tides move through it, tempering and deepening.

> There be none of Beauty's daughters
>   With a magic like thee;
> And like music on the waters
>   Is thy sweet voice to me:
> When, as if its sound were causing
> The charmed ocean's pausing,
> The waves lie still and gleaming
> And the lull'd winds seem dreaming . . .

Metrical subtleties abound. How are we to read lines 2 and 4? Their rhythm runs clean contrary to lines 1 and 2. Ocean currents cross here, move into eddies in 5 and 6, sink to rest in the quiet cove of the final couplet: it is a shorescape *felt* in its pressures and crispations more than *seen* in its moon-blanched solitude. With the second strophe we are out in mid-ocean:

> And the midnight moon is weaving
> Her bright chain o'er the deep . . .

There is a deliberate widening of the horizon, deepening of the emotion. A favourite sleeping-child image emerges, introducing the maternal element into the Virgin syndrome I have earlier noted: we pass on, consequently, to planes of 'adoration' and 'the bowed spirit' transcending the natural 'magic' of strophe one.

'So We'll Go No More A Roving' belongs to another world—no longer the 'swell of Summer's ocean' or the criss-cross of currents in a moonlit cove, though this is also a watery world, the intricate labyrinth of Venice's canals and slightly sinister 'calles'. Emotionally too we are moving through a very different spectrum. Though 'the moon be still as bright', it shines down on a subfusc world of muted gestures and responses. The scene is shadowy: human arti-facts—churches, palaces, bridges—impend over slowly-moving waters. Though never mentioned, the 'fairy city of the heart' is pervasively present. Byron here has achieved a masterpiece of non-statement.

> So, we'll go no more a roving
>   So late into the night,
> Though the heart be still as loving
>   And the moon be still as bright.
>
> For the sword outwears its sheath,
>   And the soul outwears the breast,
> And the heart must pause to breathe,
>   And love itself have rest.
>
> Though the night was made for loving,
>   And the day returns too soon,
> Yet we'll go no more a roving
>   By the light of the moon.

A cyclic poem, in its end is its beginning. A poem of disillusion, of weariness, of ambiguities. Firm rhymes—night, bright; breast, rest; soon, moon—are intercalated with imperfect rhymes—roving, loving; sheath, breathe—of which the first pair is 'feminine', the second 'masculine'. Under the ægis of the moon, the poem is encapsulated in a feminine ambience, pressing softly on the nostalgic nerve: roving, loving, heart, moon, too soon, no more. But at its centre the male weariness, lack of resilience, the sword which cannot bend but may break, asserts itself in protest.

'So . . .' The quizzical, dry, slightly mocking tone is established at the outset. We may read it with a variety of nuances. 'So . . .': *very well*; or, *is it really true?*; or, *given that, then . . .?* We have not exhausted the possibilities. The archaism 'a-roving' (about which I shall have more to say) also suggests irony, a playing down of the situation, a deliberate skirting of the absurd (for her sake, or Byron's? we don't know, but perhaps it is an echo of her voice we hear in 'So late . . .', an echo of the flirtatious beginnings of the attachment: 'Let's explore Venice . . .'—'But, darling, it's so late . .') Trivia, so far, with a touch of pathos infused from the woman's predicament. But the pattern is suddenly disturbed, and 'So late' takes on a darker significance with 'into the night'.[1] 'So late' modulates into 'Too late', 'roving into the night' becomes a perilous adventure, takes on resonances of destiny, of the human condition, Eliot's 'they are all gone into the dark'.

Eliot comes to mind again in the hint of a popular song in line 1 of the third stanza, where the banality adds a further ingredient to this complex poem, as 'The moon shone bright on Mrs Porter' does to 'The Fire Sermon'. This is a side to Byron's technique which is, or should be, acceptable to modern readers, though it made little sense to his contemporaries. Pope knew it, of course, as 'The Art of Sinking'; indispensable in a long poem, it can be effective in a short one too. In a sense, indeed, 'So We'll Go No More A Roving' as a whole is an exercise in the art of sinking. Is there a phrase in the three stanzas which is 'poetic' or 'magical', anything felicitous to set side by side with Keats's 'perilous seas' or Wordsworth's 'sovereign cry'? The poem 'sinks' into its triple context: topical, the between-the-lines ambience of palace-shadowed canals, looming churches; existential, the universal human predicament; personal, the immediate man-woman situation. Byron has achieved here that coalescence of time, place and loved one, that 'grace dissolved in place', that he sought through a thousand cruces in *Childe Harold* and the Tales; but he achieves it at the point of dissolution. The extraordinary impact of the poem, felt by every reader, depends on its being a non-poem, on its submergence in an impersonal substrate, as the effect of the grey column 'commingling slowly with heroic earth' in the earlier verse depended on its sinking out of the sphere of humanity into that of Nature.

But to discuss the poem as poetry we must return to the personal, to the immediate situation and the means by which

---

[1] A line in the original MS of *The Giaour*, replaced in the printed poem by the present line 1146, supports my 'sombre' reading of this phrase: 'That quenched, I wandered far in night'.

this is conveyed. Deeply involved, the speaker seems to withdraw; again the 'I' is absent, '*my* heart' is replaced, clinically, by '*the* heart'. We are presented with a situation which is not directly described. All that leads up to it is assumed to be understood; in this sense the poem is a private document, an entry in an erotic journal. For understanding, the poet relies on the reader's common humanity, his sharing in the existential irony. The vortex has brought these two together; now it separates them, throws them on to its outer rim, where the night is waiting to receive them. We are at the still centre, the eye of the cyclone, watching the disruptive process. Irony permits us this double stance. It is the moment of the breaking wave, the turning tide.

The poem acts as a miniature lens, a concave mirror,[1] a 'signifying glass'. It 'doesn't magnify'. Its action is by indirection, meiosis, even absurdity. Take that initial 'a-roving'. The archaism isn't simply archaic, it's rustic too, belongs to the world of minor balladry, hopelessly out of place in the baroque sophistication of Venice, as though one tootled a harpsichord theme of Vivaldi on a bamboo pipe. This 'is at least one definite false note', as Eliot puts it in his 'Portrait of a Lady', in our Venetian symphony. Within the tiny compass of the poem we move in and out of 'irony', 'absurdity', 'sincerity', 'pathos', 'cruelty', 'detachment', 'commitment', 'personality', 'impersonality'; the miniature vortex spins to the tune of these compulsions. For this is stasis in dynamis: not stagnation, not even the poised rest of 'She Walks in Beauty' or 'There be None of Beauty's Daughters', but a taut, coiled-spring nucleus of divergent forces. I see this poem as the hinge of Byron's gate from past into future.

Irony is implicit in the poem's circular structure.[2] We

---

[1] Cf. my remarks on the focusing function of *Childe Harold* in my first essays, p. 14.

[2] Circles, diagrammatizing the 'vortices', run through Byron's life and work: a circle of trees on a hill-top 'mark the spot where a story ended', his early love for Mary Chaworth; bullrings and amphitheatres are prominent in *Childe Harold*, as are 'a stern round tower of other days',

'rove', but are trapped in the circuit of our own insufficien-
cies, in the maze of Venice itself and all it stands for: the
unreal, the operatic, the overfluid. The initial 'So . . .' is
answered by the terminal 'Yet . . .' The false rhyme,
'roving–loving', 'sheath–breathe', implies an emotional
ambiguity infecting both partners. The wavering, watery
rhythms, the obliquity of phrase conveying a shared experience which yet for Byron is solitary (keeping a sceptical
corner to himself) the tone poised between acceptance and
regret—all this is sited within the amphibious city. The
sensitivity to 'this grace dissolved in place' passes here into
an inner dimension. Woman and city are not distinct.
Does the woman exist apart from the city? Cities, for Byron,
are always feminine; for Blake and Shelley they are generally
masculine, foci of tyranny. His relation to Athens (*Childe
Harold* II) was filial, the impulse was to revere and protect;
to Venice it is loverlike. If 'The spouseless Adriatic mourns
her lord' the Doge, Byron is not reluctant to comfort her
and Venice's widowhood:

> I loved her from my boyhood—she to me
> Was as a fairy city of the heart . . .

This necessity to identify himself with places, and his
emotional contacts with places, may have its origins in
Byron's own rootlessness, his lack of a 'background'; that
time, place and loved one should not only be 'together'
but fused was for him a compulsion. Hence the later
'Stanzas to the Po' and the final 'On This Day . . .'.

To savour the subtle contours of a place's, a time's or a
woman's identity was part of the Byronic sensitivity, which
left him free to be the ironic observer—yet a *spectator ab
intra*, not *ab extra*.[1] The full irony is achieved only by the
totally involved. Byron could not say, with Landor, 'I

and the Pantheon; the 'circus' of Bonnivard's cell in *The Prisoner of Chillon*
connects with the 'amphitheatre' of the besieged Ismail in *Don Juan*
VII, xxiii. Rome is 'the circus of an empire' in *The Deformed Transformed*,
I, ii, 282.

[1] The comparison is with Wordsworth: see Byron I, p. 29.

strove with none, for none was worth my strife'—almost
anything which touched humanity was worth Byron's
strife, and he struck at Izaak Walton in defence of fishes[1]
with the same fervour with which he opposed the Turks in
support of Greece. Human beings could defend themselves,
however, as fishes could not; Byron is never flippant about
wounded eagles or stags at bay. Women flummoxed him:
the long, involved ordeal of Mrs Byron, May Gray, Mary
Chaworth, Teresa Macri, London prostitutes, Annabella,
Augusta, Caroline Lamb—it was all too much. 'The sword
outwears its sheath.' No Freudian exegesis of the phrase is
necessary to let us feel the utter sexual fatigue of the middle
stanza. Here he is at the centre, the 'moment of truth'.
Here human insufficiency is set against 'romantic' demands:
the sword outwears its sheath, the heart must pause to
breathe, love itself must rest. Was there ever a 'love poem'
with such a wry admission of failure? Yet the poem exists as
a love poem. Such a success could only be sustained through
an equilibrium set up *in* the poem as artifact, *outside* the
poem as existential drama. Its existence in the poem I think
I have sufficiently demonstrated—in its close, cyclic pattern,
its skeletal, almost algebraic emotional-image structure.
Outside the poem (while implied in it) a whole time-
structure is seen to be evolving. If the middle stanza, the
moment of *present* truth, comes as a quiet explosion, the
first and third stanzas function in terms of past and future.
This is a poem of time and the heart's battle with time.
Line 1 *connects* the future—'We'll go'—with the past—
'no more'—and the present—'A-roving'; line 2 *comments*—
'So late?'—and *menaces*—'into the night'. Space adds its
ironies too: the bright moon shines down with indifferent
glamour on fragmented time and hearts. There is a bitter
antithesis in 'bright' and 'loving'—the 'cold, lunar beam'
and the warm, vulnerable heart. Anyone who has loved and
lost knows that terrible brightness of the moon. It lights up,
here, the Piranesi vistas of arcades receding into arcades,

[1] *Don Juan*, XIII, cvi.

piazzas, 'calles', canals, and the tiny human figures waving briefly to each other as the night receives them.

V. POEMS OF EXILE AND DESPAIR

The tornado exists in its motion and only there. Slowing down, it disintegrates. For Byron, as we have seen, perpetually new stimuli were required to activate the poetic nerve. Not for him the Wordsworthian feeding on old experiences, or the Shelleyan delight in 'the abstract joy'. The great lyrics are moments of temporary stasis in the universal flux, and the best of these are necessarily brief. In the poems we have just considered, the spinning top betrays no wobble, the poise is perfect, the note secure. In each, we live in the moment, and the moment contains within itself the seed of its own renewal. From the momentary stalemate of 'Oh! snatch'd away . . .' the lysis comes in the last stanza: 'Away! we know that tears are vain . . .'; in the others the imagery, the evanescence of the situation itself, warn us that soon we must be on our way to fresh woods and other pastures.

But these were poems of transition, of the hinge moment of Byron's life, when many possibilities lay open to him. As the routine of his Italian sojourn closed in upon him, we sense a lessening of emotional and intellectual tension. More and more his themes centre in situations of checkmate or stalemate—imprisonment, exile, shipwreck, the marooned sailor, the castaway. The series begins with *The Prisoner of Chillon* and ends with *The Island* and 'On this day I complete my thirty-sixth year'; it includes *The Lament of Tasso* and *The Prophecy of Dante*. Since I have just discussed the best of his lyrics, 'So We'll Go No More A Roving', I shall begin this final section of my survey with a glance at 'On This Day', a poem which has received high praise from a number of critics. It was approved of by so devout a Wordsworthian as the late Sir Herbert Read, and Arnold included it in his anthology, while rejecting 'There Be None of

Beauty's Daughters', to my mind a much finer poem.[1]
He includes it, I think, not on a 'real' but on both a 'personal'
and an 'historical' estimate[2] of its value. For Arnold, too,
liked to think of himself as a warrior making a last stand
against the Philistines:

> Charge once more, then, and be dumb!
> Let the victors, when they come,
> When the forts of folly fall,
> Find thy body by the wall!

This is the very accent of Byron's poem:

> Seek out—less often sought than found—
> A soldier's grave, for thee the best;
> Then look around, and choose thy ground,
> And take thy rest.

Or rather, let us say, one of the accents, for a very cursory
reading shows us that 'On This Day . . .' is a remarkably
confused and ill-knit document. Perhaps the immediate
circumstances of its composition have something to do with
this. Count Gamba records:

This morning Lord Byron came from his bedroom into the apartment
where Colonel Stanhope and some friends were assembled, and said
with a smile—'You were complaining the other day, that I never write
any poetry now. This is my birthday, and I have just finished something,
which, I think, is better than what I usually write.' He then produced
these noble and affecting verses.

There is something pathetic about Byron's hesitant 'pro-
duction' of the new poem, and something very uncharacter-
istic about its genesis—written to *prove* something, written
for the occasion. Birthdays were things Byron usually
passed over in grim silence. But now Byron is at the end of
his tether. The night has closed in about him; he is irre-
versibly 'the castaway', with no avenue of escape save death.

[1] I suspect, though of course it cannot be proved, that Arnold's not very
subtle ear was baffled by the poem's metrical complexity.
[2] The three estimates listed by Arnold in his essay 'The Function of
Poetry', which opens his *Essays in Criticism*, II.

The vortex is immobilized, stifled in the mud and muddle of Missolonghi. Byron is frustrated at every turn, deprived on the one hand of that fruitful solitude which sustained his reflective centre, and on the other of the action, the significant gesture which would fulfil his historic destiny. 'Byron . . . Byron . . . Byron', he had scrawled over the page of *Childe Harold* which posed his own prophetic questions:

> Fair Greece! sad relic of departed worth!
> Immortal, though no more; though fallen, great!
> Who now shall lead thy scatter'd children forth,
> And long accustomed bondage uncreate . . .
> Oh! who that gallant spirit shall resume,
> Leap from Eurotas' banks, and call thee from the tomb?
>
> (II,lxxiii)

And 'Byron' is still the answer in that strand of the present poem which projects the Byronic *will*, the gesture towards fulfilment in action:

> The sword, the banner, and the field,
> Glory and Greece, around me see!
> The Spartan, borne upon his shield,
> Was not more free.

Yet even here, with all the dash and daring of the rhetoric, we discern a collapse, a contradiction. That Spartan, sad relic of departed Harrow schooldays, what is he doing here? I do not query him simply as a faded classical 'property', for which presumably Byron would have got a rap over the knuckles from Dr Drury, but as an *in any way* meaningful support of Byron's stance. The Spartan soldier, however noble, is a *dead* soldier, and what Greece needs at this juncture is living soldiers, and shields as defences, not as stretchers. The trope is not even neat: in what sense is the Spartan free—and 'more free' than whom? In what context? This collapse of meaning-structure infects the whole poem; on inspection we find it is not one poem, but two, very clumsily glued together, and with no necessary connexion with each other.

Poem 1 consists of verses i to iv, and viii; poem 2 of

verses vi, vii, ix and x. Verse v is an awkward join. The first poem is plaintively amatory:

> 'Tis time this heart should be unmoved,
>> Since others it has ceased to move:
> Yet, though I cannot be beloved,
>> Still let me love.

The whine is unpleasant; the second thoughts implant a seed of disruption in the poem from the outset. Worse is to follow.

> My days are in the yellow leaf;
>> The flowers and fruit of love are gone;
> The worm, the canker, and the grief
>> Are mine alone!

That Byron has to fall back upon Shakespeare, so early in so short a poem is ominous; and now we are in full botanical spate: leaf, flowers, fruit, worm, canker—'Solitary Grief' by 'Twelfth Night' out of 'Macbeth'!

> The fire that on my bosom preys
>> Is lone as some volcanic isle;
> No torch is kindled at its blaze—
>> A funeral pile.

From fruit, worms and cankers we are wrenched into another set of clichés: fires, islands, torches, volcanoes, funeral pyres. He is plagiarizing his own *Sardanapalus* and

> 'The cold in clime are cold in blood
>> Their love can scarce deserve the name;
> But mine was like the lava flood
>> That boils in Ætna's breast of flame'.

>> (1099-1102)

from *The Giaour*. Compare the resilience of that (however 'crude' we may judge it to be) with the limp defeatism of this last poem. And the defeat is critical as well as emotional: only a year earlier Byron had laughed at his volcanoes in a witty stanza of *Don Juan*:

> I hate to hunt down a tired metaphor,
>> So let the often-used volcano go.
> Poor thing! How frequently, by me and others,
> It hath been stirr'd up till its smoke quite smothers!
>
>> (XIII, xxxvi)

That is a Byron still in possession of his faculties of humour and self-criticism. In the next stanza of 'On this day . . .' we are confronted with a Byron who has sustained the final defeat: an inarticulate Byron!

> The hope, the fear, the jealous care,
>> The exalted portion of the pain
> And power of love, I cannot share,
>> But wear the chain.

Presumably this means something; to know *what* demands a long footnote, which Byron does not give us. The alliteration (and alliterations on the letter *p* are rarely effective outside a comic setting) does not reassure. We wonder what is the *un*-exalted portion of the pain and power of love —does he 'share' that? Do we (Lord Mayors aside) ever 'wear' a chain? The stanza is a muddle, and our minds may well revert to the Venice lyric with its brilliant turning to account of an unexplained situation as the polar opposite of this unfortunate poem.

Limply abandoning its cankered fruits and volcanic isles, the lyric sags back into a self-pitying complaint. Stanza v is a joiner and a bracer, ludicrous in its determined tightening of the upper lip.

> But 'tis not *thus*—and 'tis not *here*—
>> Such thoughts should shake my soul, nor *now*,
> Where glory decks the hero's bier,
>> Or binds his brow.

And it's still all wrong. Italics—that bane of Byron's poetry —try to compensate for the lack of internal stress. The counters are false tender: shaken souls, bound brows, hero's biers. How could this sort of thing be accepted by critics of the eminence of Arnold and Sir Herbert Read as genuine currency? The answer, if I have got it right, is interesting. You start off with the recognition of Byron as a major poet, of *some* sort; you know he is a 'Romantic' poet; you do not like the side of him that is not 'Romantic'; you ferret out the bits that are *something* like Wordsworth or Shelley, blow them up, turn a blind eye to their defects, and hey presto! here is your respectable 'Romantic' Byron. Grateful anthologists bring up the rear.

Poem 2 now begins:

> The sword, the banner, and the field,
> Glory and Greece, around me see!
> The Spartan, borne upon his shield
> Was not more free.
>
> Awake! (not Greece—she *is* awake!)
> Awake, my spirit! Think through *whom*
> Thy life-blood tracks its parent lake,
> And then strike home!

'Awake, my spirit!', he says. But to awake it must hark back to old dynastic arrogances, to his mother's reputed descent from Kings of Scotland—and this brings him up against something much stronger than repute, the still-living, still-torturing mother-son antagonisms of his childhood. And once again the attempted surge outwards, into freedom, into action, is cramped by ancient fetters.

With stanza viii we are back in poem 1:

> Tread those reviving passions down,
> Unworthy manhood!—unto thee
> Indifferent should the smile or frown
> Of beauty be.

The reviving passions were homosexual—probably for Loukas, the last of those 'little pages' who were always so picturesque a feature of Byron's wanderings over the Mediterranean scene. War and love, his old antitheses, engage in a final tussle here: for a moment Achilles, sulking in his tent over Patroclus, focuses a fading vignette of a Harrow schoolroom. The theme affords an unconvincing modulation into poem 2. But all is poorly realized, argumentative, fussily petulant:

> If thou regrett'st thy youth, *why live?*
>   The land of honourable death
> Is here: — up to the field, and give
>   Away thy breath!
>
> Seek out — less often sought than found —
>   A soldier's grave, for thee the best;
> Then look around, and choose thy ground,
>   And take thy rest.

The first line seems to mean: If the urge to revert to boyhood is so strong that life as an adult is hardly worth living, why not end it all? Better perish in battle. It is not a very heroic compulsion. That a soldier's grave might be best for Byron is a personal judgement on which it is useless to comment. That a soldier on the battlefield has it in his power to look around and choose his ground, whether for fighting or dying, is so improbable as to verge on the ludicrous, and the jingle of the internal rhyme adds a music-hall touch.

Byron's final lyric[1] is an extreme case of what happens to his writing when the integrating vortex-into-vortex spin is suspended. I could bring forward other examples from among his later lyrics—but what is the point of analysing bad poems? A handful of longer poems—not bad, and meriting our critical attention—close the reflective-elegiac-prophetic roster for this penultimate epoch of his career. In these too the same suspension of energy, the same failure of nerve, may be traced. All are projections of the 'castaway' syndrome.[2] All are identifications—with Bonnivard, with Mazeppa, with Tasso, with Dante. But they are voluntary identifications—in the Missolonghi lyric the horrid reality had been forced upon him. Yet in Byron's 'circle of destiny'

[1] Or last but one. Professor Marchand thinks the lines beginning 'I watched thee when the foe was at our side' are the last Byron wrote.

[2] I shall continue to use this term as shorthand for the complex of imprisonment, rejection, abandonment, isolation and despair images in Byron's work from now on. A re-reading of Cowper's remarkable poem 'The Castaway' may help the reader's understanding.

we may discern the Missolonghi entrapment as the lethal, negative centre of the maelstrom, exerting its pull from the beginning, a 'black hole' in 'the eternal space' into which the castaway is being sucked from the days of his earliest gyrations on the outer rim, the days of Newstead, Harrow, Cambridge, and the Pilgrimage, when 'freedom'—from his early life, from morality, from society, from himself—seemed poised on the next turn of the vortex.

I have already had something to say in my first essay about *The Prisoner of Chillon* and *Mazeppa*, Byron's first projections of the castaway. *The Lament of Tasso* (1817) is a closer identification; Tasso himself is a poet, his imprisonment is (reputedly) for love and means a deprivation of love, he has been judged to be mad by his oppressors.

> Long years! — It tries the thrilling frame to bear
> And eagle-spirit of a Child of Song —
> Long years of outrage, calumny, and wrong;
> Imputed madness, prison'd solitude,
> And the mind's canker in its savage mood,
> When the impatient thirst of light and air
> Parches the heart; and the abhorred grate,
> Marring the sunbeams with its hideous shade,
> Works through the throbbing eyeball to the brain
> With a hot sense of heaviness and pain . . .   (1–10)

The vortex is spinning here: the long, involved sentence gyrates through its intricacies of rhyme from the freedoms of 'eagle-spirit' and 'Child of Song' down through a narrowing funnel to the 'hideous shade', the 'throbbing eyeball' and the 'hot sense of heaviness and pain'. This is splendid, but the trouble is that it can be done, with effect, only once in a poem: the pattern suits a sonnet, but sets an impossible standard of intensity for a longer work. The rhyme-scheme is admirably fitted to the feverish, involuted, semi-delirious mood of the poem: like the striations in the inner wall of a rapidly-spinning funnel, the rhymes unfold, interlace, separate, come together again, with vertiginous effect: a, b, b, c, c, a, d, e, f, f . . . and so on for the thirty-two lines of the first section. If we are tempted, as we are in watching the interlacing striations in such a spinning funnel, to impose a pattern of regular rhyming (say in groups of six: a, b, b, c, c, a) we shall find the symmetry deceptive; Byron's strophe development is genuinely long term. Each of the nine sections of the poem is a 'bolge'[1], a funnel spinning at speed. If we think of the rhymes in terms of their vowel sounds only, the use of recurrence is even more striking: in section 1 we have only six terminal sounds, in which long *a*, long and short *i*, and long and short *o* predominate. This reinforces the obsessive effect. If this could have been kept up the result would have been a masterpiece. But the triumph is self-destructive, like continuing to watch a sunset or smell a rose. After strophe 1, we find our attention waning.

Nevertheless, *The Lament of Tasso* makes its point as a profoundly moving diagram of pain and frustration. If it is not a great *poem*, but rather what Coleridge called 'Kubla Khan', 'a psychological curiosity', the fault lies partly, as I have suggested, in the very special skill shown by Byron in devising a structural pattern adequate to his emotion but not to the development in verse of that emotion, and partly in the absence from its 'world' of those elements—light, air, sunshine, mountains, the sea—which I have already suggested, perhaps *ad nauseam*, to be ingredients of success for Byron. For lack of outside friction, the spin slows down disastrously towards the close of the poem.

As though conscious of this, Byron introduces in section vi an excursus which removes the axis of the poem from the dungeon to the air of freedom, and in doing so opens up one of his favourite fields of speculation. Tasso is thinking of the power of love to 'foil the ingenuity of Pain':

> It is no marvel—from my very birth
> My soul was drunk with love—which did pervade
> And mingle with whate'er I saw on earth:
> Of objects all inanimate I made
> Idols, and out of wild and lonely flowers,

[1] Referring to the 'bolges' or pits in the eighth circle of Dante's *Inferno*.

And rocks, whereby they grew, a paradise,
Where I did lay me down within the shade
Of waving trees, and dream'd uncounted hours,
Though I was chid for wandering; and the Wise
Shook their white aged heads o'er me, and said
Of such materials wretched men were made,
And such a truant boy would end in woe,
And that the only lesson was a blow . . .   (149-61)

A fascinatingly Blakean passage, which brings us nearer,
one suspects, to the boy Byron at Aberdeen or Harrow than
to the boy Tasso at Sorrento. And in 'drunk with love', in
the connexion of the erotic with 'objects all inanimate',
we are back with the Byron of *Childe Harold* III who feels that

All is concenter'd in a life intense,
Where not a beam, nor air, nor leaf is lost . . .   (lxxxix)[1]

Significant for our understanding of Byron, the passage
breaks for a moment (but only to emphasize) Tasso's bitter
realization of his predicament. The contrast between the
willed solitude of childhood days and the enforced loneliness
of prison, between a love expanded through the universe
and a passion feeding on itself—

Dwelling deep in my shut and silent heart,
As dwells the gather'd lightning in its cloud,
Encompass'd with its dark and rolling shroud,
Till struck—forth flies the all-ethereal dart!   (113-16)

—brings Tasso to thoughts of madness and suicide (sections
viii and ix), the 'final solution' of Byron's tragic heroes from
Manfred to Sardanapalus. He resists, upheld by the dream
of fame. Within the poem's structure these conflicting
motives constitute a mainspring, replace to some degree the
outer thrust, keep the poem in motion, but cannot compensate, in Byron's poetry, for the fruitful intercourse of inner
and outer, the cosmic dynamism.

[1] See *Byron I*, p. 29; and my *The Lost Travellers*, p. 68n.

The Prophecy of Dante was written at Ravenna in June 1819 on a visit to Teresa Guiccioli. 'Being deprived at this time of his books, his horses, and all that occupied him at Venice', Teresa naively records, 'I begged him to gratify me by writing something on the subject of Dante; and, with his usual facility and rapidity, he composed his *Prophecy*.' Byron himself described the poem, in a letter to John Murray, as 'the best thing I have ever done, if not *unintelligible*'. Byron had not much in common with Wordsworth, but a total absence of the critical faculty connects them, as far as their own writings are concerned: *The Prophecy of Dante* is not the best thing Byron ever did. Nor is it 'unintelligible'. We can read in it, all too clearly, the initial stages of Byron's lapse into the morbidities, self-pitying compulsions, and self-destructive urges which culminated in 'On this day I complete my thirty-sixth year'.

Byron's veneration for 'the great Poet-Sire of Italy', as he calls him in his Dedicatory Sonnet, was of long standing. His 'childish amour' for Mary Duff (Journal, 26 Nov. 1813) chimed with Dante's love for Beatrice; the Italian poet's unhappy marriage and exile were a paradigm of his own.[1] Dante's popularity with his own countrymen reminded him of his own contemporary fame (Journal, 29 Jan. 1821). Questioning Wordsworth's contention 'that *no* great poet ever had immediate fame; which being interpreted, means that William Wordsworth is not quite so much read by his contemporaries as might be desirable',[2] he points out that 'Dante's Poem was celebrated long before his death; and, not long after it, States negotiated for his ashes, and disputed for the sites of the composition of the *Divina Commedia*'. We must remember too that among modern poets it was Dante who embodied the classical and European values so essential for Byron, as for Arnold, as a counterpoise to Shakespeare.

[1] Cf. *Don Juan*, III,x,xi.
[2] 'Observations upon an Article in Blackwood's Magazine' (Ravenna, 1820).

Dante, then, is a living voice speaking from the past. Homer, Virgil, Horace, Sappho are voices speaking from the past (and precious voices for Byron) but they are not living voices. Shakespeare is a living voice (and precious for Byron) but he does not speak from the past. Living in Italy, Byron felt himself in direct contact with this magisterial utterance, a presence linked through Virgil with the ancient world and through tradition with the modern. He can merge himself in its flux. This is important for Byron, a poet who always speaks out of a mobile context (while other poets seek to anchor themselves) of 'what is past, and passing, and to come'. That Dante is a Christian and indeed a theological poet hardly matters for Byron, who has the wit anyway to penetrate behind the doctrinal carapace neither (accepting nor rejecting it)[1] to the archetypal verities it expresses. I suspect too that he sensed Dante's other roots in the Islamic, Sufic civilization which had come to mean so much to him in his earlier wanderings.[2] I believe that if Byron had lived he would have opened himself more and more to the influence of Dante. For here he found, disciplined, controlled, the 'bolgic' stresses behind his own output. Here he found patterned energy.

All this being said, one records with regret that *The Prophecy of Dante* is not a success. Put crudely, there is too much Byron, too little Dante. And it is Byron in his worst, his self-pitying, world-cursing *persona*. Initially, one expects a triumph. The poem begins well, with Dante emerging from the tremendous other-worldly experience of the *Divina Commedia*:

> Once more in man's frail world! which I had left
> So long that 'twas forgotten; and I feel
> The weight of clay again—too soon bereft
> Of the immortal vision which could heal
> My earthly sorrows . . .   (I. 1-5)

---

[1] Byron's religious beliefs (or superstitions) are a complex subject.
[2] Recent researches have shown the considerable penetration of Islamic thought into *La Divina Commedia* and other works of Dante.

The metrical form too, the *terza rima*, with its interlacing rhymes, might be expected to give scope for what I have called the 'mobile context' of Byron's *weltanschauung*. But the trouble is that this is not a mobile Dante. This is Byron's version of a defeated, an exiled Dante. A disagreeably nagging tone swiftly asserts itself. Through the mouth of Dante, Byron voices his own frustration, bitterness, thirst for revenge. The immediacy of Tasso's situation, in the earlier poem, is absent: the dungeon, the tyrant, the lost love; and we do not feel for Dante the human sympathy we have for Tasso. A dungeon is one thing, exile another.

Tasso's dungeon is a powerful 'objective correlative' in the earlier poem; Byron attempts to give Dante as useful a one in his image of the marooned sailor towards the close of Canto I:

> For I have been too long and deeply wreck'd
> On the lone rock of desolate Despair
> To lift my eyes more to the passing sail
> Which shuns that reef so horrible and bare:
> Nor raise my voice—for who would heed my wail?
>
> (I,138–42)

but 'deeply wreck'd' is a bad phrase, and 'wail' is an insult to the stern grandeur of Dante. Self-pity is contaminated with the revenge obsession, so tiresome a feature of the auto-biographical Byron:

> . . . my lone breast may burn
> At times with evil feelings hot and harsh,
> And sometimes the last pangs of a vile foe
> Writhe in a dream before me, and o'erarch
> My brow with hopes of triumph—let them go! (I, 105–9)

This is fustian, and exploitation. And though the poem picks up somewhat in the succeeding cantos, where Dante's prophetic vision, ranging through the centuries, lists one by one the catastrophes which will afflict Italy and Europe, even here the obsessional, nagging note persists.

In his 'Stanzas to the Po', another poem of 1819 and like *The Prophecy* written at Ravenna, Byron strikes a more assured note. It was written 'in red-hot earnest', he says in a letter of 8 June 1820 to Hobhouse, but there is nothing fervid about it. Indeed it is a curiously impersonal poem; It opens with a cluster of tired archaisms: 'the lady of my love', 'perchance', 'faint and fleeting memory', but improves in its second stanza:

> What if thy deep and ample stream should be
> A mirror of my heart, where she may read
> The thousand thoughts I now betray to thee,
> Wild as thy wave, and headlong as thy speed!

It is a poem *to* Teresa, but *about* Byron, and if 'The Dream' was his 'Tintern Abbey', this is his approach to the Immortality Ode (or, more closely, to Coleridge's 'Dejection'). For it is a threnody, a lament for vanished powers, for decayed passions. These were once as tumultuous as the Po, but now

> Time may have somewhat tamed them—not for ever[1]
> Thou overflow'st thy banks, and not for aye
> Thy bosom overboils, congenial river!
> Thy floods subside, and mine have sunk away:
>
> But left long wrecks behind, and now again,
> Borne on our old unchanged career, we move:
> Thou tendest wildly onwards to the main,
> And I—to loving *one* I should not love.   (13-20)

The Wordsworth-Coleridge æsthetic—'I see, not feel, how beautiful they are'— is here transposed into the Byronic passional: 'Such as thou art were my passions long'. But the tone is muted, Arnoldian rather than Byronic or Wordsworthian. And in later stanzas, we find ourselves, bewilderingly, in Marvell's world:

> But that which keepeth us apart is not
> Distance, nor depth of wave, nor space of earth,
> But the distraction of a various lot,
> As various as the climates of our birth.

---

[1] The semi-colon printed at the end of this line is clearly a mistake.

The poem is, then, an oddity. In his one and only river poem, Byron seems to be fishing, rather desultorily, for new possibilities, new bearings. But its final stanza points directly to Missolonghi.

> 'Tis vain to struggle—let me perish young—
>   Live as I lived, and love as I have loved;
> To dust if I return, from dust I sprung,
>   And then, at least, my heart can ne'er be moved.

That a nerve has failed, that Byron has lost his way, that a lobotomy is being operated on the complex structure we have explored in *Childe Harold*, and the Tales: these are different ways of saying the same thing. However we phrase it, it seems clear to me that Byron in his brief development goes the same road, from spiritual riches to impoverishment, trod by Wordsworth and Coleridge in their longer pilgrimage. But he covers it up. He can do this because of the reservoir of pure energy he still harbours within himself. The energy is there, but the channels in which it used to flow are silting up. In the dramas, in *Beppo* and *Don Juan*, Byron will open new channels to his daemonic drive: but they will be shallower, narrower than before. The regression is clear in *Don Juan* itself, where the first seven cantos have a richness and zest absent from the later ones, which rely on cleverness and flippancy for their effects.

We can push this diagnosis a bit further. The later Byron is the castaway, but he is so because he is now the fragmented Byron. At some point in the years of transition—perhaps at the moment when he clutched at the prospect of happiness with Annabella—Byron broke his link with the All. He is no longer, in the later poems, the Byron to whom 'high mountains *are* a feeling', who lives through these stony extensions of his human senses. In the poems of exile and despair he is the outcast. In the dramas and long poems of the final period—in *Don Juan*, *The Island*, and even in *The Vision of Judgment*—he is the split man; and as such we shall go on to consider him in the next essay.

BYRON

A Select Bibliography

(Place of publication London, unless stated otherwise. Detailed bibliographical information will also be found in the appropriate volume of
The Cambridge Bibliography of English Literature and *The Oxford History
of English Literature*.)

Bibliography:

THE LIFE OF LORD BYRON, by Hon. R. Noel (1890)
—includes *Bibliography* by J. P. Anderson, containing extensive lists
of magazine articles about Byron and of musical settings.

A BIBLIOGRAPHY OF SUCCESSIVE EDITIONS AND TRANSLATIONS in *The
Works of Lord Byron. Poetry*, Vol. VII (1904), ed. E. H. Coleridge
—the best general bibliography of the poems.

BYRON IN ENGLAND, by S. C. Chew (1924)
—contains an extensive list of Byroniana.

BIBLIOGRAPHICAL CATALOGUE of the First Editions, Proof Copies and
Manuscripts of Books by Lord Byron. Exhibited at the First
Edition Club, January 1925 (1925).

A DESCRIPTIVE CATALOGUE OF . . . MANUSCRIPTS AND FIRST EDITIONS . . .
AT THE UNIVERSITY OF TEXAS, ed. R. H. Griffith and H. M. Jones;
Austin, Texas (1924).

BYRON AND BYRONIANA. A Catalogue of Books (1930)
—an important sale catalogue, valuable for reference, issued by Elkin
Mathews, the London booksellers.

A BIBLIOGRAPHY OF THE WRITINGS IN VERSE AND PROSE OF GEORGE
GORDON NOEL, BARON BYRON. With Letters illustrating his Life and
Work and particularly his attitude towards Keats, by T. J. Wise,
2 vols (1932-3)
—the standard analytical bibliography. Incorporates the material of
the same author's *A Byron Library*, 1928, the privately printed
catalogue of the Byron Collection in the Ashley Library, now in
the British Museum.

THE ROE-BYRON COLLECTION, Newstead Abbey; Nottingham (1937)
—the catalogue of the collection at Byron's ancestral home.

Note: The archives of John Murray, Byron's publishers, at 50
Albemarle Street, London, contain important manuscript material.

Collected Works:

THE POETICAL WORKS, 2 vols; Philadelphia (1813)

—the first collected edition, followed throughout the nineteenth century by numerous other collected editions in several volumes, published in London, Paris, New York, and elsewhere.

THE WORKS, 4 vols (1815)

—new editions, 1818-20 (8 vols); 1825 (8 vols); 1831 (6 vols).

THE WORKS, with His Letters and Journals, and His Life, by Thomas Moore, ed. J. Wright, 17 vols (1832-3).

THE POETICAL WORKS. New Edition, with the Text Carefully Revised, 6 vols (1857).

THE POETICAL WORKS, edited, with a Critical Memoir by W. M. Rossetti. Illustrated by Ford Madox Brown, 8 vols (1870).

THE WORKS. A New, Revised, and Enlarged Edition with Illustrations, including Portraits, 13 vols (1898-1904)

—*Poetry*, ed. E. H. Coleridge, 7 vols; *Letters and Journals*, ed. R. H. Prothero, 6 vols.

THE POETICAL WORKS. The Only Complete and Copyright Text in one volume. Edited with a Memoir, by E. H. Coleridge (1905)

—the standard edition, often reprinted.

Selections:

A SELECTION FROM THE WORK OF LORD BYRON, edited and prefaced by A. C. Swinburne (1866).

POETRY OF BYRON, chosen and arranged by M. Arnold (1881).

POEMS, ed. H. J. C. Grierson (1923).

THE SHORTER BYRON . . . , chosen and edited by E. Rhys (1927).

THE BEST OF BYRON, ed. R. A. Rice; New York (1933).

DON JUAN AND OTHER SATIRIC POEMS, ed. L. I. Bredvold; New York (1935).

CHILDE HAROLD'S PILGRIMAGE AND OTHER ROMANTIC POEMS, ed. S. C. Chew (1936).

SATIRICAL AND CRITICAL POEMS, ed. J. Bennett; Cambridge (1937).

BYRON, POETRY AND PROSE. With essays by Scott, Hazlitt, Macaulay, etc. With an introduction by Sir A. Quiller-Couch and notes by D. Nichol Smith (1940).

SELECTIONS FROM POETRY, LETTERS AND JOURNALS, ed. P. Quennell (1949).

Separate Works:

FUGITIVE PIECES [Newark, 1806]

—privately printed and anonymous. Facsimile reprint, ed. H. B. Forman, 1886.

POEMS ON VARIOUS OCCASIONS; Newark (1807)

—privately printed and anonymous.

HOURS OF IDLENESS: A Series of Poems Original and Translated; Newark (1807).

POEMS ORIGINAL AND TRANSLATED; second ed. of *Hours of Idleness*; Newark (1808)

—contains five new pieces.

ENGLISH BARDS AND SCOTCH REVIEWERS: A Satire [1809]

—the early editions of this poem were frequently counterfeited.

ADDRESS WRITTEN BY LORD BYRON. The Genuine Rejected Addresses, Presented to the Committee of Management for Drury Lane Theatre: Preceded by that written by Lord Byron and adopted by the Committee (1812).

CHILDE HAROLD'S PILGRIMAGE: A Romaunt. Cantos I and II (1812); Canto III (1816); Canto IV (1818); Cantos I-IV were collected in 2 vols (1819).

THE CURSE OF MINERVA: A Poem (1812).

WALTZ: An Apostrophic Hymn 'by Horace Hornem, Esq.' (1813).

THE GIAOUR: A Fragment of a Turkish Tale (1813).

THE BRIDE OF ABYDOS: A Turkish Tale (1813).

THE CORSAIR: A Tale (1814).

ODE TO NAPOLEON BUONAPARTE, [Anon] (1814).

LARA: A Tale (1814).

HEBREW MELODIES, Ancient and Modern with appropriate Symphonies and Accompaniments (1815).

THE SIEGE OF CORINTH: A Poem. PARISINA: A Poem, [Anon] (1816).

[POEMS ON HIS DOMESTIC CIRCUMSTANCES] (i. Fare Thee Well. ii. A Sketch from Private Life) (1816)

—these two poems had been privately printed and separately printed in the same year. Various editions of this collection with additional poems were published in 1816.

POEMS (1816).

THE PRISONER OF CHILLON AND OTHER POEMS (1816).

MONODY ON THE DEATH OF THE RIGHT HON. R. B. SHERIDAN. Written at the Request of a Friend, to be Spoken at Drury Lane (1816).

THE LAMENT OF TASSO (1817).

MANFRED: A Dramatic Poem (1817).

BEPPO: A Venetian Story (1818). Anonymous

—fourth ed., with additional stanzas, 1818.

MAZEPPA: A Poem (1819).

DON JUAN. Cantos I and II (1819); Cantos III, IV, V (1821); Cantos VI, VII, VIII (1823); Cantos IX, X, XI (1823); Cantos XII, XIII, XIV (1823); Cantos XV, XVI (1824) originally published anonymously.

—first collected edition, 2 vols, Edinburgh 1825; ed. T. G. Steffan and W. W. Pratt, 4 vols, Austin, Texas 1957; (the fullest edition, of which Vol. I contains a detailed study of the composition of the poem).

MARINO FALIERO, DOGE OF VENICE: An Historical Tragedy. THE PROPHECY OF DANTE: A Poem (1821).

SARDANAPALUS: A Tragedy. THE TWO FOSCARI: A Tragedy. CAIN: A Mystery (1821).

THE VISION OF JUDGMENT (1822)

—a product of Byron's feud with Southey, first printed in *The Liberal*, 1822, an ephemeral paper promoted by Byron and Leigh Hunt. Published as *The Two Visions* with Southey's 'Vision of Judgment' in the same year.

HEAVEN AND EARTH: A Mystery, [Anon] (1823).

—first printed in *The Liberal*, 1823.

THE AGE OF BRONZE: Or, Carmen Seculare et Annus haud Mirabilis, [Anon] (1823).

THE ISLAND: Or, Christian and His Comrades (1823).

WERNER: A Tragedy (1823).

THE PARLIAMENTARY SPEECHES OF LORD BYRON. Printed from the Copies prepared by his Lordship for Publication (1824).

THE DEFORMED TRANSFORMED: A Drama (1824).

Diaries, Letters, etc.

LETTER TO [John Murray] ON THE REV. W. L. BOWLES' STRICTURES ON THE LIFE AND WRITINGS OF POPE (1821).

CORRESPONDENCE OF LORD BYRON WITH A FRIEND, including his Letters to his Mother in 1809-11, ed. A. R. C. Dallas, 3 vols; Paris (1825).

LETTERS AND JOURNALS OF LORD BYRON, with Notices of his Life, by T. Moore, 2 vols (1830, revised edition 1875).

LETTERS AND JOURNALS, ed. R. E. Prothero, 6 vols (1898-1904).

POEMS AND LETTERS, edited from the original MSS in the possession of W. K. Bixby, by W. N. C. Carlton; privately printed, Chicago (1912).

LORD BYRON'S CORRESPONDENCE, chiefly with Lady Melbourne, Mr Hobhouse, the Hon. Douglas Kinnaird, and P. B. Shelley, ed. John Murray, 2 vols (1922).

SELECTED LETTERS, ed. V. H. Collins; Oxford (1928).

THE RAVENNA JOURNAL, mainly compiled at Ravenna in 1821, with an Introduction by Lord Ernle [R. E. Prothero] (1928)

—printed for the members of the First Edition Club.

LETTERS, ed. R. G. Howarth with an Introduction by André Maurois (1933).

BYRON LETTERS AND DIARIES: A SELF PORTRAIT, ed. P. Quennell, 2 vols (1950)

—the largest and best selection of Byron's correspondence, including many hitherto unpublished letters.

BYRON: HIS VERY SELF AND VOICE, ed. E. J. Lovell (1954)

—a collection of Byron's conversation.

Some Critical and Biographical Studies:

A JOURNEY THROUGH ALBANIA AND OTHER PROVINCES OF TURKEY, by J. C. Hobhouse (1813).

HISTORY OF A SIX WEEKS' TOUR, by P. B. Shelley (1817).

MEMOIRS OF THE LIFE AND WRITINGS OF THE RT. HON. LORD BYRON, with Anecdotes of Some of his Contemporaries, by [J. Watkins] (1822).

JOURNAL OF THE CONVERSATIONS OF LORD BYRON: Noted during a Residence with his Lordship at Pisa, in the Years 1821 and 1822, by T. Medwin (1824).

NOTES ON CAPTAIN MEDWIN'S CONVERSATIONS OF LORD BYRON, by John Murray; privately printed (1824)

—reprinted in *Works*, 1829.

RECOLLECTIONS OF THE LIFE OF LORD BYRON, from the Year 1808 to the End of 1814, by R. C. Dallas (1824).

THE SPIRIT OF THE AGE, by W. Hazlitt (1825)

—contains an essay on Byron.

A NARRATIVE OF LORD BYRON'S LAST JOURNEY TO GREECE, by Count P. Gamba (1825).

ANECDOTES OF LORD BYRON FROM AUTHENTIC SOURCES, by [Alexander Kilgour] (1825).

THE LAST DAYS OF LORD BYRON: With his Lordship's Opinions on Various Subjects, particularly on the State and Prospects of Greece, by Major W. Parry (1825).

NARRATIVE OF A SECOND VISIT TO GREECE, including Facts connected with the Last Days of Lord Byron, Extracts from Correspondence, Official Documents, etc., ed. Edward Blaquiere (1825).

THE LIFE, WRITINGS, OPINIONS AND TIMES OF THE RT HON. GEORGE GORDON NOEL BYRON, LORD BYRON, by an English Gentleman in the Greek Military Service, and Comrade of his Lordship. Compiled from Authentic Documents and from Long Personal Acquaintance, 3 vols (1825)
—ascribed to the publisher, Matthew Iley.

LORD BYRON AND SOME OF HIS CONTEMPORARIES, by Leigh Hunt (1828).

THE LIFE OF LORD BYRON, by J. Galt (1830).

CONVERSATIONS ON RELIGION WITH LORD BYRON AND OTHERS, by J. Kennedy (1830).

MEMOIRS OF THE AFFAIRS OF GREECE, with Various Anecdotes Relating to Lord Byron, and an Account of his Last Illness and Death, by J. Millingen (1831).

CONVERSATIONS OF LORD BYRON WITH THE COUNTESS OF BLESSINGTON, by Marguerite Gardiner, Countess of Blessington (1834).

CRITICAL AND HISTORIC ESSAYS, by T. B. Macaulay (1842)
—includes review of *Letters and Journals of Lord Byron; with Notices of his Life*, by T. Moore, 1830.

LECTURES ON THE ENGLISH POETS, by W. Hazlitt (1858).

RECOLLECTIONS OF THE LAST DAYS OF SHELLEY AND BYRON, by E. J. Trelawny (1858; ed. E. Dowden, 1906)
—see also the same author's *Records of Shelley, Byron, and the Author*, 2 vols, 1878, new eds. 1887, 1905.

LORD BYRON JUGÉ PAR LES TÉMOINS DE SA VIE, by Countess T. Guiccioli, 2 vols (1868)
—English translation, 1869.

MEDORA LEIGH: A History and An Autobiography, by E. M. Leigh, ed. C. Mackay (1869).

A CONTEMPORARY ACCOUNT OF THE SEPARATION OF LORD AND LADY BYRON: Also of the Destruction of Lord Byron's Memoirs, by J. C. Hobhouse; privately printed (1870)
—reprinted in Hobhouse's *Recollections of a Long Life*.

BYRON, by J. Nichol (1880)
—in the *English Men of Letters* series.

THE REAL LORD BYRON: New Views of the Poet's Life, by J. C. Jeaffreson, 2 vols (1883).

BYRON RE-STUDIED IN HIS DRAMAS. An Essay, by W. Gerard [Smith] (1886).

ESSAYS IN CRITICISM, by M. Arnold, 2nd series (1888).

THE LIFE OF LORD BYRON, by the Hon. R. Noel (1890).

LAST LINKS WITH BYRON, SHELLEY AND KEATS, by W. Graham (1898).

JOURNAL OF EDWARD ELLERKER WILLIAMS, Companion of Shelley and Byron in 1821 and 1822. With an Introduction by R. Garnett (1902).

ASTARTE: A Fragment of Truth concerning Lord Byron, by Ralph Milbanke, Earl of Lovelace; privately printed (1905)
—enlarged edition, published 1921.

LORD BYRON AND HIS DETRACTORS. 'Astarte. Lord Byron and Lord Lovelace', by Sir J. Murray; 'Lord Lovelace on the Separation of Lord and Lady Byron', by R. E. Prothero (1906)
—privately printed for members of the Roxburghe Club.

BYRON: THE LAST PHASE, by R. J. F. Edgcumbe (1909).

RECOLLECTIONS OF A LONG LIFE, by J. C. Hobhouse (1909-11).

THE DIARY OF DR JOHN WILLIAM POLIDORI, relating to Byron, etc.
—edited and elucidated by W. M. Rossetti (1911).

LORD BYRON AS A SATIRIST IN VERSE, by C. M. Fuess (1912).

BYRON, by E. Colburn Mayne, 2 vols (1912, new ed. 1924)
—see also the same author's The Life and Letters of Lady Noel Byron, 1929.

LORD BYRON'S ILLNESS AND DEATH as described in a Letter to the Hon. Augusta Leigh, dated from Missolonghi April 20, 1824, by W. Fletcher; privately printed, Nottingham (1920).

THE RELATIONS OF LORD BYRON AND AUGUSTA LEIGH. With a Comparison of the Characters of Byron and Shelley. Four letters by E. J. Trelawny; privately printed (1920).

BYRON IN ENGLAND: His Fame and After Fame, by S. C. Chew (1924).

BYRON: THE LAST JOURNEY, April 1823-April 1824, by the Hon. Harold Nicolson (1924)
—new ed. 1948.

BYRON IN PERSPECTIVE, by J. D. Symon (1924).

BYRON, THE POET. A Centenary Volume, ed. W. A. Briscoe (1924)
—contains essays by Haldane, Grierson and others.

THE BACKGROUND OF ENGLISH LITERATURE, by H. J. C. Grierson (1925)
—contains 'Byron and English Society'.

LA FORTUNA DI BYRON IN INGHILTERRA, by M. Praz; Florence (1925)
—see also The Romantic Agony, translated A. Davidson, 1933.

ALLEGRA: The Story of Byron and Miss Clairmont, by A. C. Gordon; New York (1926).

THE HAUNTED CASTLE, by E. Railo (1927).

BYRON, ET LE BESOIN DE LA FATALITÉ, by C. Du Bos; Paris (1929)
—English translation by E. Colburn Mayne, 1932.

LORD BYRON: PERSÖNLICHKEIT UND WERK, by H. Richter (1929).

BYRON, by André Maurois, 2 vols; Paris (1930)
—English translation by H. Miles, 1930.

BYRON: THE YEARS OF FAME, by P. Quennell (1935).

ALLEGRA, by I. Origo (1935).

BYRON: ROMATIC PARADOX, by W. J. Calvert (1935).

REVALUATION, by F. R. Leavis (1936)
—contains his influential essay 'Byron's Satire'.

FROM ANNE TO VICTORIA, ed. B. Dobrée (1937)
—contains 'Byron' by T. S. Eliot, reprinted in *On Poetry and Poets*, 1957.

BYRON AS SKEPTIC AND BELIEVER, by E. W. Marjarum; Princeton, N.J. (1938).

TO LORD BYRON: Feminine Profiles, Based upon Unpublished Letters 1807-1824, by G. Paston and P. Quennell (1939).

'Byron and the East: Literary Sources of the Turkish Tales', *Nineteenth Century Studies*, ed. H. Davies, W. C. de Vane and R. C. Bald (1940).

BYRON IN ITALY, by P. Quennell (1941).

BYRON'S DON JUAN, by E. F. Boyd (1945).

LORD BYRON'S FIRST PILGRIMAGE, by W. A. Borst; New Haven, Conn. (1948).

BYRON: THE RECORD OF A QUEST, by E. J. Lovell; Austin, Texas (1949).

THE LAST ATTACHMENT. The Story of Byron and Teresa Guiccioli, by I. Origo (1949).

GOETHE AND BYRON, by E. M. Butler (1951).

THE TRUE VOICE OF FEELING, by Sir H. Read (1951)
—contains an essay on Byron.

LORD BYRON, CHRISTIAN VIRTUES, by G. W. Knight (1952).

FAIR GREECE, SAD RELIC: Literary Philhellenism from Shakespeare to Byron, by T. Spencer (1954).

BYRON AND GOETHE, by E. M. Butler (1956).

LORD BYRON, UN TEMPÉRAMENT LITTÉRAIRE, by R. Escarpit; Paris (1956-7).

THE PELICAN GUIDE TO ENGLISH LITERATURE, Vol. V, ed. B. Ford (1957)
—contains 'Lord Byron', by J. D. Jump.

MAJOR ENGLISH ROMANTIC POETS, ed. C. D. Thorpe (1957)
—includes 'Irony and Image in Byron's Don Juan'.
BYRON, by L. A. Marchand, 3 vols (1957)
—the standard life.
THE METAMORPHOSES OF DON JUAN, by L. Weinstein (1959).
ON POETRY AND POETS, by T. S. Eliot (1959)
—contains an essay on Byron, first published in 1937.
BYRON AND THE SPOILER'S ART, by P. West (1960).
THE STYLE OF DON JUAN, by G. M. Ridenour; New Haven (1960)
—Yale Studies in English, Vol. CXLIV.
THE LATE LORD BYRON, by D. L. Moore (1961).
BYRON, by A. Rutherford (1961).
THE LOST TRAVELLERS, by B. Blackstone (1962)
—contains a chapter expanded from 'Guilt and Retribution in Byron's Sea Poems', in *A Review of English Literature*, Vol. II, January 1961.
LORD BYRON'S WIFE, by M. Elwin (1962).
THE BYRONIC HERO, by P. L. Thorster, Jr; Minnesota (1962).
THE STRUCTURE OF BYRON'S MAJOR POEMS, by W. J. Marshall; Philadelphia (1962).
BYRON: A Collection of Critical Essays, ed. P. West; Englewood Cliffs (1963).
BYRON THE POET, by M. K. Joseph (1964).
BYRON AND SHAKESPEARE, by G. Wilson Knight (1966).
FIERY DUST: BYRON'S POETIC DEVELOPMENT, by J. J. McGann; Chicago (1968).
THE JOURNALS OF CLAIRE CLAIRMONT, ed. M. K. Stocking; Cambridge, Mass. (1969).

Note: Reference should also be made to the following Nottingham Byron Foundation Lectures: *Byron's Lyrics*, by L. C. Martin (1948); *Byron and Switzerland*, by H. Straumann (1948); *Byron and Shelley*, by D. G. James (1951); *Byron's Dramatic Prose*, by G. Wilson Knight (1953); *Two Exiles: Lord Byron and D. H. Lawrence*, by G. Hough (1956; reprinted in *Image and Experience*, 1960); *Byron and Italy*, by G. Melchiori (1958); *Byron and the Greek Tradition*, by T. Spencer (1959); and *Byron's Dramas*, by B. Dobrée (1962).